MUSEUM OF ANTHROPOLOGY, THE UNIVERSITY OF MICHIGAN

TECHNICAL REPORTS

Number 8

RESEARCH REPORTS IN ARCHAEOLOGY

Contribution 4

LATE PREHISTORIC BISON PROCUREMENT IN SOUTHEASTERN NEW MEXICO: THE 1977 SEASON AT THE GARNSEY SITE

by

John D. Speth
William J. Parry

ANN ARBOR
1978

ISBN 978-0-932206-73-2 (print)

ISBN 978-1-951538-39-2 (ebook)

TABLE OF CONTENTS

LIST OF ILLUSTRATIONS

LIST OF TABLES

APPENDIX I. BISON REMAINS FROM THE GARNSEY SITE

LIST OF TABLES

ACKNOWLEDGMENTS

The Bureau of Land Management (BLM) has been extremely helpful to us in all stages of our research at the Garnsey site. In particular, we would like to acknowledge the assistance given the project by Mr. James H. O'Connor, District Manager of the BLM for the Roswell District, New Mexico; and also the assistance provided by Ms. Ann Ramage, District Archaeologist for the BLM, also in Roswell. We are especially grateful to Mr. Leo Flynn, BLM archaeologist in Santa Fe, New Mexico, for notifying us of the existence and potential importance of the site and for his continuing encouragement and interest. We also are grateful to Mr. Dan Harrison of Roswell who brought the site to the attention of the BLM.

We also would like to acknowledge the kindness and generosity of Elmer and Jane Garnsey, local ranchers who lease the land on which the site is located from the BLM. They have shown considerable interest in the project and have been extremely helpful in innumerable ways. The site has been named in their honor.

Several specialists have given freely of their time and knowledge. These include Richard I. Ford (Ethnobotany and Palynology), William R. Farrand (Geology), Jeffrey and Mary Parsons (Archaeology) and David and Cordelia Thomas Snow (Archaeology).

The members of the crew were excellent, and we are truly grateful for their help. Those who participated for most or all of the season included Katherine Spielmann, Mark King, Katherine Moynes, Karen Mudar, Elissa Warantz and Joan Howe. During the month of June, we benefitted immeasurably from the assistance of Jeffrey and Mary Parsons and Alfred Speth.

Penelope Pate, Jennie Neumann and Melinda Fertig have been very helpful in the analysis of the bison remains, assisting in various stages of the work from restoration and labeling to measurement and interpretation.

Finally, we would like to express our gratitude to Mary Hodge and Katherine Spielmann for their invaluable help in preparing and editing the manuscript, to George Stuber for providing photographs of several of the archaeological specimens, and to other members of the University of Michigan Museum of Anthropology staff who assisted in the preparation of the report.

Financial support for the project was provided by generous grants from the Museum of Anthropology and from the Horace H. Rackham School of Graduate Studies (Faculty Research Grant No. 387269), both of the University of Michigan.

1. INTRODUCTION

This report presents the preliminary results of the first season of excavation conducted at the Garnsey site in Southeastern New Mexico under Federal Antiquities Act Permit No. 77-NM-037. The primary objectives of this project were to establish the archaeological nature of bones exposed in the walls of an actively eroding arroyo, to determine the approximate age of these remains and to gain some preliminary insight into the nature of the prehistoric activities they represent.

The investigations of the first season demonstrated that the Garnsey site was indeed archaeological. The bones were those of modern bison (*Bison bison*) and were the remains of a series of kill events dating to the late prehistoric and early historic periods. Bison kills of this age have not previously been investigated in New Mexico, despite the abundant ethnohistoric documentation of the importance of bison in Pueblo subsistence and ritual and despite the frequent recovery of bison remains from prehistoric and historic Pueblo ruins (cf. White 1942; Reed 1955). Similarly, few kills of this age have been investigated elsewhere in the Southern Plains, although there too, bison remains have been recovered in considerable quantity from late prehistoric and historic campsites and villages (Dillehay 1974; Greer 1976).

The Garnsey site therefore offers the potential of providing valuable insights into the role of bison procurement in the subsistence and settlement systems of late prehistoric and early historic groups in and adjacent to the western margins of the Southern High Plains. In particular, analysis of the Garnsey site should complement studies of bison remains from campsites and villages, providing information on the technology of procurement, methods of processing, seasonal timing of procurement activities and so forth.

Moreover, the bison remains from the Garnsey site, including the skulls, are relatively well preserved. Analysis of these remains provides a useful corpus of data that may be compared systematically with contemporary materials from elsewhere in the Plains. Such comparisons contribute to an understanding of the degree and nature of geographical variation in the skeletal morphology of modern bison and ultimately form an important component of studies concerned with the evolution of the bison during the Holocene.

The principal objective of this report is to make available, as rapidly as possible, the results of the first season of excavation at the Garnsey site. Included in the report is an extensive appendix providing detailed measurements on all of the bone material recovered to date. It should be kept in mind, however, that this report is preliminary in nature. The interpretations and conclusions reached in the present study may require substantial revision as analysis progresses on the material already recovered and as new data are obtained in forthcoming fieldwork.

2. SITE DESCRIPTION

The Garnsey site is located about 12 mi. (20 km) southeast of Roswell, Chaves County, New Mexico (Fig. 1). The site is situated on Bureau of Land Management land, approximately 0.3 mi. (0.6 km) due east of the southeast corner of Bottomless Lakes State Park (SW¼ of the SW¼ of the SW¼ of Section 35, T. 11 S., R. 26 E., Bottomless Lakes 7.5 Minute Quadrangle, Topographic Series) (Fig. 2).

The wash that contains the Garnsey site (henceforth referred to as the Garnsey Wash) is one of many similar, dry washes along the eastern edge of the Pecos Valley that drain westward from a low divide at the Llano Estacado or Cap Rock (Kelley 1971). The terrain between the Llano and the Pecos, known as the Mescalero Pediment, has relatively little relief until one reaches the margin of the valley where the pediment terminates in sheer cliffs, often approaching 100 ft. in height. The bedrock exposed in these cliffs (Permian Artesia Group) consists of alternating beds of red, brown and green siltstones and extensive layers of grayish gypsum (Kelley 1971). Along the base of the cliffs and cutting deeply into them are seven large, circular or oval sinkholes, filled with deep, freshwater lakes. Six of the lakes are included within the Bottomless Lakes State Park. The seventh and southernmost, Dimmitt Lake, is privately owned.

The mouth of the Garnsey Wash opens into the Pecos Valley near the southeast boundary of the Park, between Dimmitt and Lea Lake. The site itself is located about 400 to 500 m upstream from the mouth. The wash in the area of the site is relatively broad (up to 50 m wide), flat-bottomed and bounded by 10- to 15-m high bedrock walls. The average slope of the walls of the wash in most places is between 10° and 25°, and exceeds 45° only for very short stretches. At no place does the slope become vertical for distances of more than a few meters or for heights of more than 1 to 2 m.

The bison remains are exposed in the walls of a modern arroyo that is actively incising the alluvial filling of the wash. Arroyo-cutting was initiated less than 30 years ago by nearby highway construction (NM 409 or Park Road) that blocked the original westward flow of the wash into Lea Lake and diverted it southward into Dimmitt Lake, thereby shortening and steepening the gradient (William R. Farrand, personal communication; confirmed by New Mexico State Highway Department, Roswell District). This recent arroyo has cut a channel that in places is over 4 m deep and up to 10 m wide. An estimated 50% to 60% of the site already has been destroyed by the arroyo, and erosion continues at a rapid rate. The subsurface deposits in the Garnsey Wash have become visible only as a result of the rather unusual situation created by highway construction, and bison remains have been encountered in these deposits. It seems highly probable, therefore, that similar remains exist in the alluvial fillings of other major drainages in the area. This possibility will be investigated in forthcoming fieldwork.

2. SITE DESCRIPTION

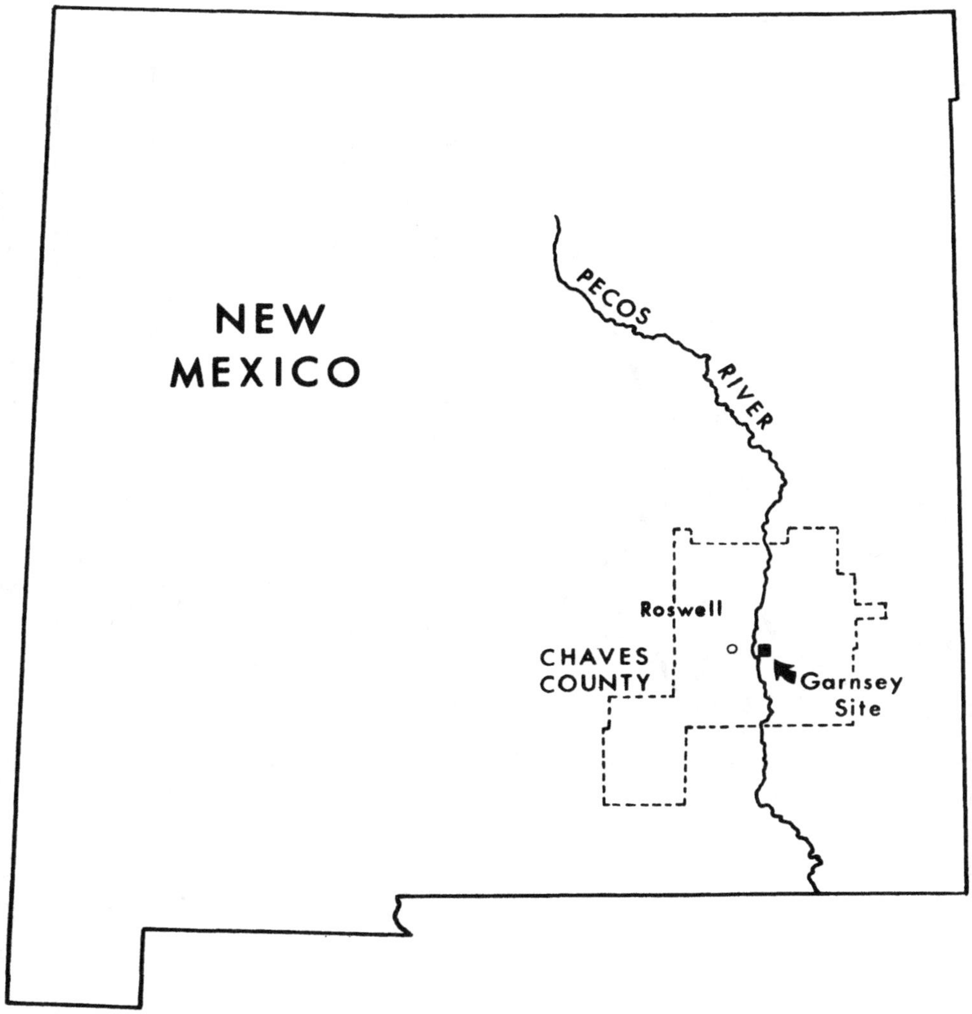

Fig. 1. Location of Garnsey site in southeastern New Mexico.

2. SITE DESCRIPTION

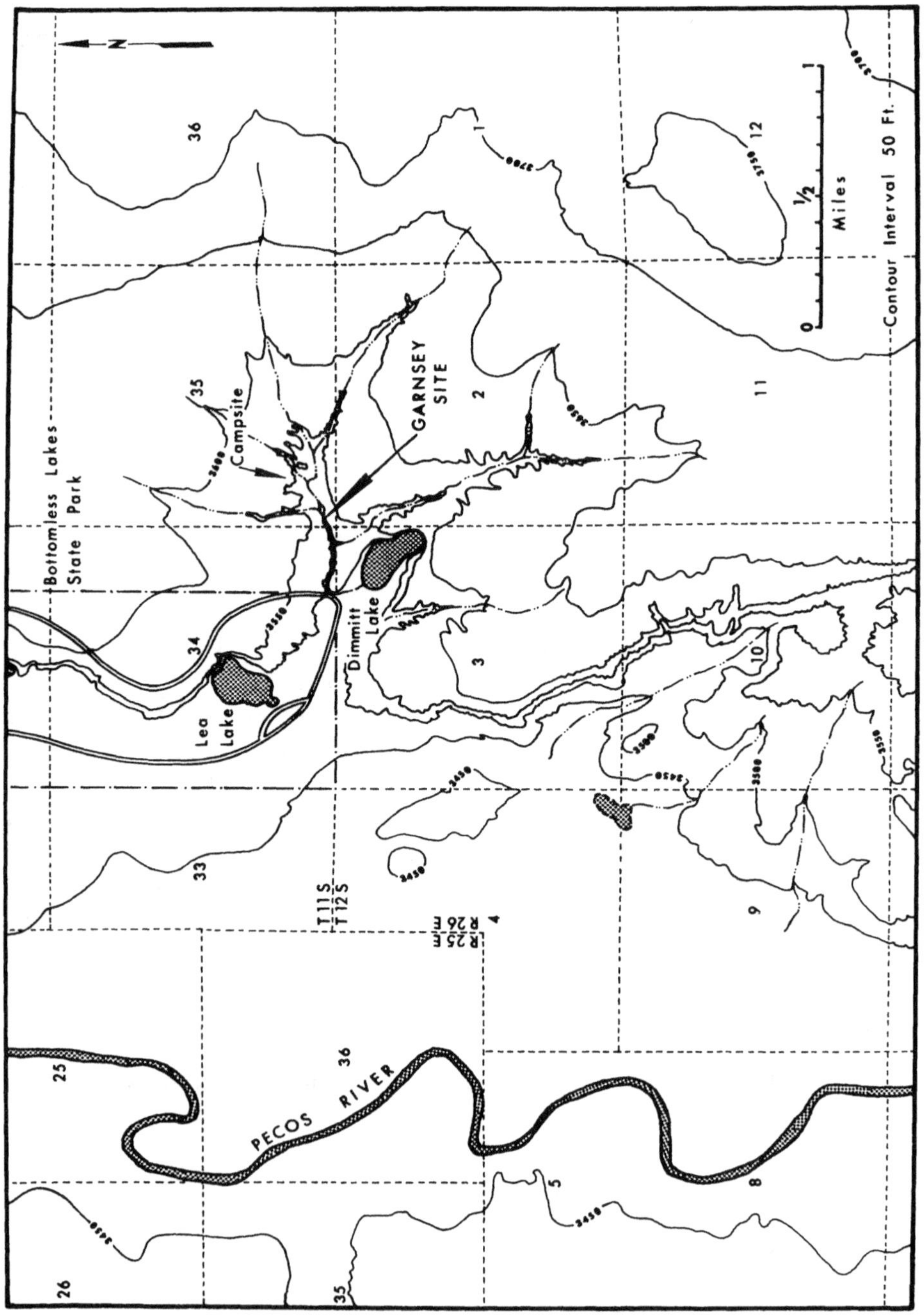

Fig. 2. Bottomless Lakes area, New Mexico, showing location of Garnsey site (adapted from USGS Bottomless Lakes 7.5 Minute Quadrangle, Topographic Series).

2. SITE DESCRIPTION

The wash today remains dry throughout most of the year. Water occasionally surges through the arroyo in the form of flash floods after particularly heavy downpours in the spring and late summer. Standing water seldom remains in the arroyo for more than a few days after a flood. Permanent freshwater is available at nearby Dimmitt Lake and also at a spring that seeps from a low bedrock scarp in the wash about 300 m east of the site. The water from the spring supports a fairly lush growth of grasses and trees in its immediate vicinity, but none of the water remains on the surface for more than a few meters downstream.

The vegetation in the wash today undoubtedly has been altered rather drastically by the arroyo-cutting. The floor of the wash is covered with a relatively sparse growth of sacaton (*Sporobolus* sp.) and other grasses, and mesquite (*Prosopis* sp.) (Fig. 3). Other washes in the area that have not been incised by recent erosion support much denser stands of grasses. This is nicely illustrated by Comanche Wash, located only about 4 mi. (7 km) north of the Garnsey Wash (Fig. 4).

Fig. 3. General view of Garnsey Wash and modern arroyo, facing southwest (south wall of Dimmitt sinkhole visible in background).

2. SITE DESCRIPTION

Fig. 4. Modern vegetation in undissected Comanche Wash.

The majority of bison bones exposed in the walls of the arroyo at the Garnsey site form a thin, irregular and discontinuous layer that varies from 1.2 to about 1.7 m below the surface of the wash. At no point do the remains occur in concentrations approaching the quantities of bone encountered in jump or trap sites in the Northern Plains (cf. Reher 1977). Moreover, bones are not entirely confined to this single layer. Some bison remains occur at shallower depths, but seldom less than about 40 to 50 cm below the surface.

Beginning at the mouth of the wash and progressing upstream, bones first appear in the deposits several meters east of the prominent tributary that enters the wash from the south, just to the east of Dimmitt Lake (Fig. 2). For convenience, we will refer to this as the East Dimmitt Wash. From this point onward, bison bones occur in very low densities in both walls of the arroyo. Beginning about 30 m east of the boundary between Sections 34 and 35 (T. 11 S., R. 26 E.) and continuing for at least 50 m, the density of bone in the walls of the arroyo increases markedly. It is also at this point, though no relationship is apparent, that the arroyo reaches its greatest depth. The excavations of the 1977 field season focused on this area of the wash. Continuing upstream, the bottom of the arroyo rises abruptly nearly 2 m over a bedrock sill and then becomes rapidly shallower and narrower as one progresses upstream toward the spring. Bison remains decrease in both walls but continue to occur for at least another 50 m. By this point the floor of the arroyo is less than a meter below the surface of the wash, and if bison bones are present, they are not yet exposed. The arroyo disappears completely before reaching the spring, and the remainder of the wash is undissected.

Before turning to a more detailed discussion of the Garnsey site, two other archaeological occurrences in the immediate area deserve mention. A small campsite is located on the terrace above the main wash, about 400 m northeast of the 1977 excavations and 150 m north-northeast of the spring (Fig. 2). This site consists of a shallow surface midden 20 to 25 m in diameter and perhaps only 10 to 15 cm in depth. Artifacts on the surface, in addition to some historic materials, include considerable quantities of lithic debitage, brownware ceramics and fragments of projectile points. This site will be examined in detail during the 1978 field season.

Fig. 5. Bichrome red and black pictograph near spring in Garnsey Wash (scale in centimeters).

2. SITE DESCRIPTION

About 50 m east-northeast of the spring, in an overhang formed in the north wall of the main wash, are several monochrome red, and bichrome red and black pictographs (an example is provided in Fig. 5). They are in poor condition, due both to the extremely soft and corrodable surface on which they have been executed and to the destructive proclivities of vandals.

3. METHODOLOGY

The area of the site was surveyed using an alidade and plane table, and a detailed contour map was prepared (Fig. 6). The site was gridded in 1-meter units. These units were designated by a combination of letters (A, B, C, ..., etc. from "north" to "south") and numbers (1, 2, 3, ..., etc. from "east" to "west"). As excavation progressed, it became clear that the site was considerably larger than originally anticipated, and the letter-number system became cumbersome and inadequate. As a consequence, a more flexible system will be employed in subsequent fieldwork.

A total of 120 m^2 was excavated to an average depth of 2 m. The main excavation focused on the deposits on the north side of the modern arroyo (98 m^2). The particular location selected for these preliminary investigations was dictated by two major considerations: (1) It was clear from the arroyo exposures that this area would yield a sample sufficient for radiocarbon analyses, studies of the type of bison represented, and assessment of the suitability and importance of the site for more extensive investigations. (2) Nearly a half-dozen bison skulls were eroding from the arroyo walls at this location. The skulls were rapidly deteriorating and being lost by undercutting and collapsing of the arroyo walls; and they also were being removed, and in the process destroyed, by local collectors. In light of the extreme importance of cranial material for determining the species, age, sex, season of death and population structure of the bison in a kill, it was deemed imperative that the initial excavations be located in such a manner that these skulls would be salvaged.

It is clearly recognized that the material recovered in 1977 does not constitute a statistically unbiased sample of the entire site. The preliminary sample was designed to resolve certain specific questions concerning the age of the site, its state of preservation and its importance for understanding the role of bison procurement in local subsistence-settlement systems. Patterns that emerge from this initial sample concerning the sex and age structure of the kill population and the systematic removal of certain preferred parts of the carcasses may not reflect the values of these parameters in the site as a whole. The problems of defining site boundaries and of obtaining an adequate and representative sample of the site will be addressed specifically in forthcoming fieldwork.

Excavation proceeded by natural stratigraphic levels, determined according to geological and archaeological criteria. The depth below datum (Z-coordinate) was measured with a Berger Level for all cultural and faunal material. Measurements were taken to the underside of each specimen. It was felt that these values would most closely approximate the surface on which the specimens were deposited. Backplotting of Z-coordinates in the laboratory has facilitated greatly the reconstruction of microstratigraphic relationships that are independent of the stratigraphic units employed during the excavation (cf. Wobst 1975). Dip and orientation of specimens also were recorded; these are proving to be extremely useful for recognizing items that have been disturbed or transported by runoff subsequent to their initial deposition.

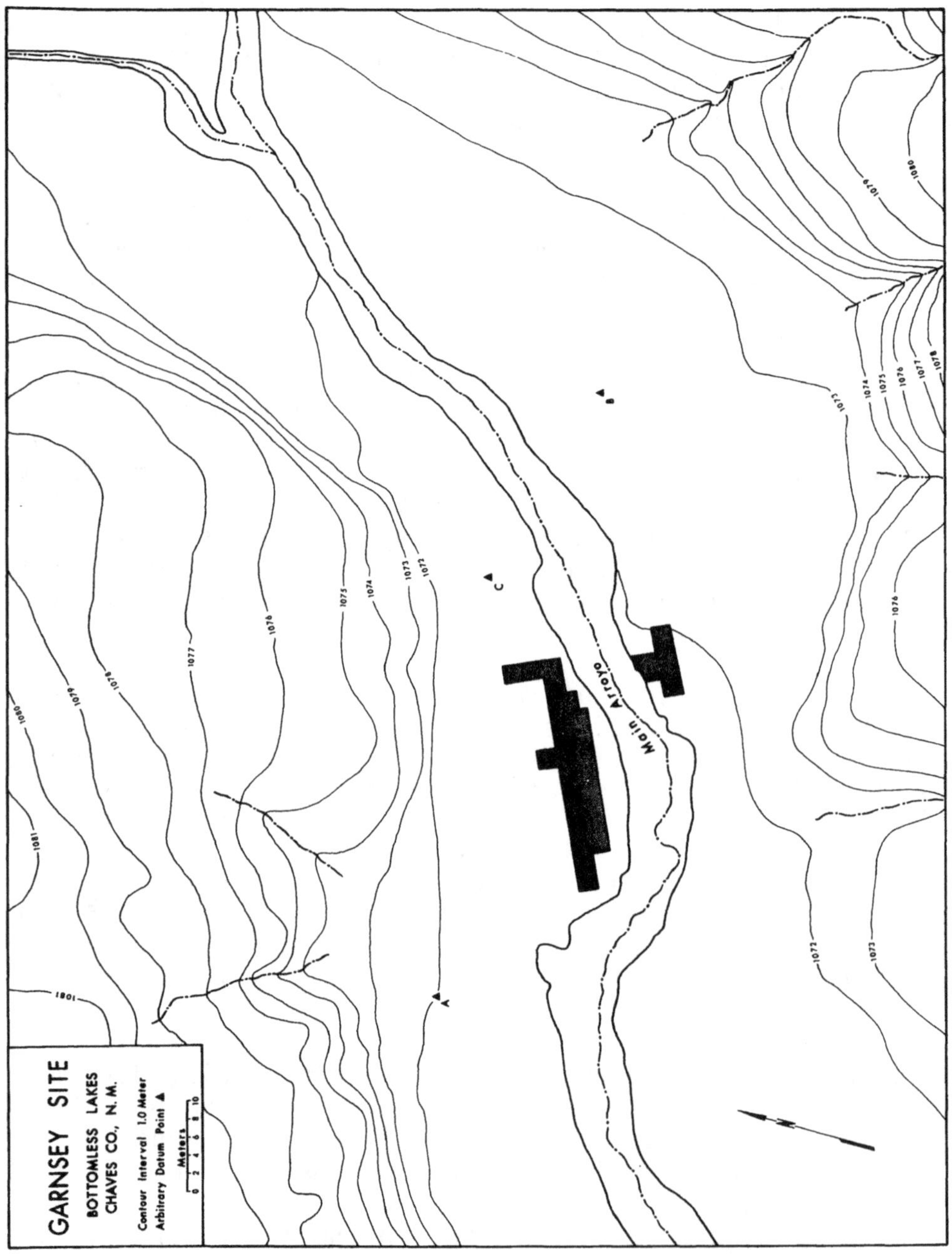

Fig. 6. Garnsey site, showing areas excavated in 1977 (A, B and C are datum points).

3. METHODOLOGY

Particular emphasis in the analysis of the Garnsey site is being placed on the spatial distribution and patterns of association of archaeological materials. All items were mapped in three-dimensional space and assigned sequential identification numbers prior to removal. These data currently are being analyzed to determine the spatial organization of kill and butchering activities. Maps are being prepared to show the distribution of specific butchering elements (e.g., axial units, appendicular units), retouch and resharpening flakes, concentrations of splintered and broken bone, and so forth. These data will provide the basis for determining the manner in which the bison were dismembered and which parts were removed from the kill area for additional processing and transport to a camp or other settlement.

All sediments from the levels yielding bone, and approximately 10 % of the sediments from non-archaeological levels,were fine-screened. This was essential in order to recover the lithic material, much of which consisted of tiny retouch and resharpening flakes (median weight 0.24 g). Sedimentological samples were collected from several complete profiles, and these currently are being analyzed by the Laboratory of Geology at the University of Michigan.

4. STRATIGRAPHY

The stratigraphy of the Garnsey site is relatively complex, and a great deal of work remains to be done before a comprehensive discussion of the depositional history and paleoenvironmental setting of the site can be presented. The synthesis which follows should be regarded as preliminary and subject to revision.

More than 4.5 m of alluvial and colluvial deposits are exposed in the walls of the arroyo immediately adjacent to the trenches excavated in 1977. At the top of the sequence, approximately the upper 1.0 to 1.2 m, the sediments consist of relatively fine, reddish-brown alluvial silt and fine to medium sand. Below these finer sediments, from about 1.2 to 1.7 m, the deposits become considerably coarser. At the east end of the main trench, at least three distinct, graded beds of alluvial and colluvial sediments can be distinguished. The basal gravel of each bed consists of poorly sorted, subangular pieces of gypsum, averaging about 1 to 2 cm in diameter. A few larger pieces of gypsum, up to 5 to 10 cm in diameter, also occur (William R. Farrand, personal communication).

In plan, the gravels are concentrated along the flanks, and particularly along the bottoms, of shallow channels. These channels, averaging about 2 m in width and perhaps 30 to 60 cm in depth, were the principal drainages on the floor of the wash at the time the gravels were deposited. Two adjacent and nearly parallel channels were traced from east to west in the main excavation on the north side of the arroyo. These are shown in section in Figure 7. The northernmost channel followed the "EF" units, becoming difficult to trace at the extreme west end of the excavation. The southern channel, at the east end of the excavation, appears to have been situated where the modern arroyo is now located. Downstream, this channel shifted slightly northward into Units G and H, converging on the "EF" channel. By Units EFGH-14, the two channels were side-by-side. The "GH" channel also becomes difficult to trace at the west end of the excavation. A third channel may have existed further south, adjacent to the excavations on the south side of the arroyo. Only the southern flank of this channel remains, in Units OP-2, 3 and 4. Other channels may exist in areas of the wash that have not been excavated.

The chronological relationships among the channels are not clear. They all may be more or less contemporary and reflect a braided drainage pattern on the floor of the wash. It is also possible, however, that they developed sequentially by lateral shifts of the drainage system.

Most of the bison remains and cultural materials are associated with these gravel deposits, particularly with the lower and middle beds. Bison were killed and butchered in and adjacent to the channels, and their remains, along with various lithic artifacts, became incorporated in the bank and channel-bottom sediments (Fig. 8). Flooding undoubtedly disturbed the bones and artifacts, but observations on the geology (William R. Farrand, personal communication) and on the spatial distribution and condition of the archaeological materials, suggest that the amount of disturbance is relatively

Fig. 7. Main excavation on north side of arroyo (facing southwest), showing "EF" and "GH" channels in section, west wall of Units EFGH-14 (prominent bulk in background).

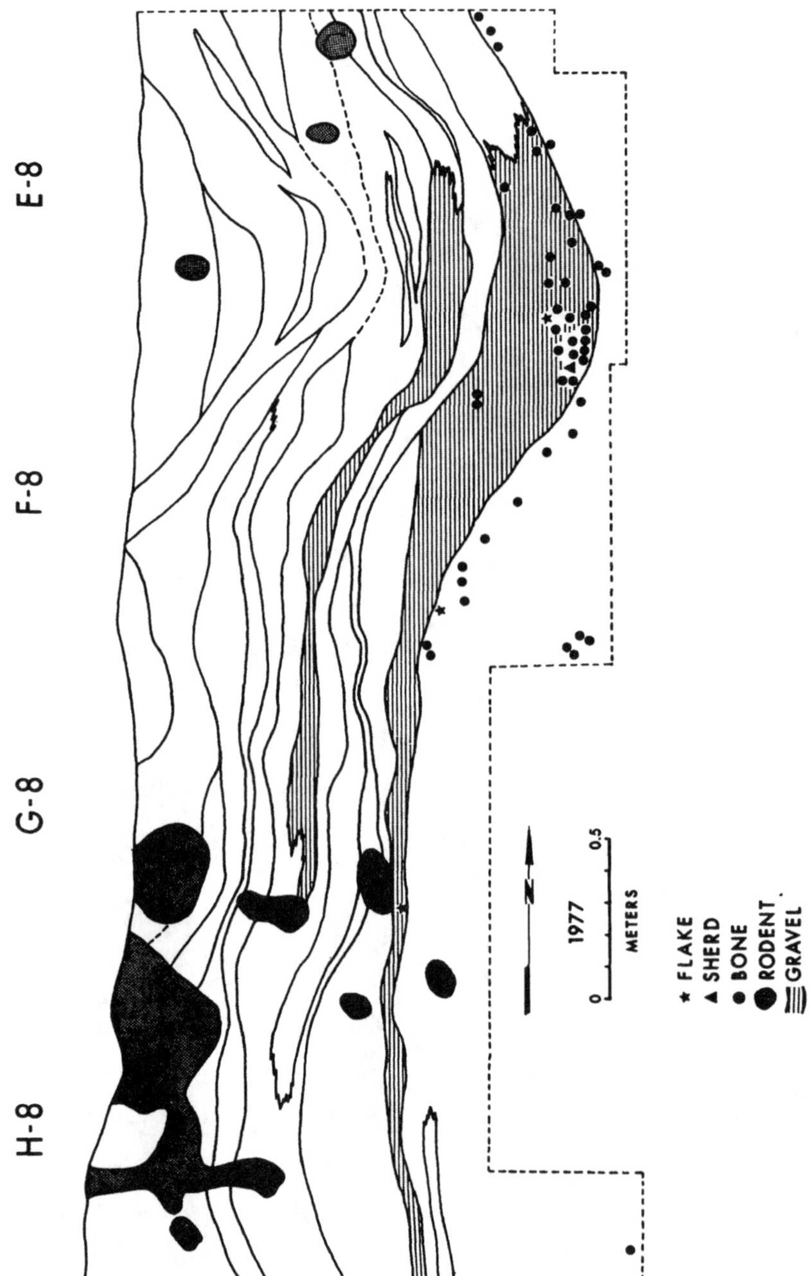

Fig. 8. "EF" channel in section, west wall of EFGH-8, showing association of bison bones and artifacts with bank deposits and channel-bottom gravels (positions of artifacts and bones in Units EFGH-8 have been projected on to section).

small, and that large-scale, long-distance transport and sorting are not major problems.

The bison remains occurred spatially in distinct clusters or concentrations, separated from each other by zones with few or no remains (Fig. 9). The precise stratigraphic relationships among the clusters, as among the channels, are not completely clear. The majority of bison bones, forming four or five large concentrations in the lower part of the gravels, may be contemporary, or nearly so. These clusters are found in Units E-1,2; EF-8,10 and G-11; H-14 and H-16, 18; and OP-2,4 and Q-4 (Fig. 9). There are scattered bison bones, however, higher up in the sequence. Conceivably, some of these remains may have been reworked from earlier deposits farther upstream. Most however probably are chronologically younger. Clarifying the stratigraphic relationships among kill events is a priority in forthcoming fieldwork.

Three radiocarbon dates have been run thus far, in an attempt to establish the age of the bison remains at the Garnsey site. These dates are summarized in Table 1. Adequate charcoal samples were not recovered in the 1977 excavations. Thus, all three dates were run on bone. The determinations were made by Geochron Laboratories in Cambridge, Mass. Dates were run on bone gelatin, with corrections made for C-13 fractionation. One of the samples (GX-5098-G) provided a very young date. As a check on this result, the lab also determined the age using bone apatite. This specimen, as noted in a footnote in Table 1, was contaminated with preservative used to stabilize an overlying skull. The date therefore is not reliable and should be rejected.

Table 1. Radiocarbon dates from the Garnsey site (1977)

Prov.	[a]Lab. No.	[b]Age	[c]Age	[d]Age
[e]O-4/13	GX-5098-A	Modern	Modern	---
[e]O-4/13	GX-5098-G	AD 1845±100	AD 1842±100	---
P-2/27	GX-5097-G	AD 1560±130	AD 1548±130	AD 1450
P-3/55	GX-5099-G	AD 1460±110	AD 1445±110	AD 1410

[a]Geochron Laboratories; A (Bone Apatite); G (Bone Gelatin).
[b]Old (Libby) half-life (5570 years).
[c]New half-life (5730 years).
[d]MASCA correction (Ralph et al. 1973); standard deviation omitted.
[e]This specimen was situated in close proximity to a skull that required considerable stabilization with preservative (Elmer's glue). Although care was taken to avoid contamination of specimens under and adjacent to the skull, radiocarbon sample O-4/13 unfortunately came in contact with glue. The date therefore is not reliable and should be rejected. More extensive radiocarbon determinations on materials obtained in forthcoming fieldwork will provide a far more secure chronological framework for the site.

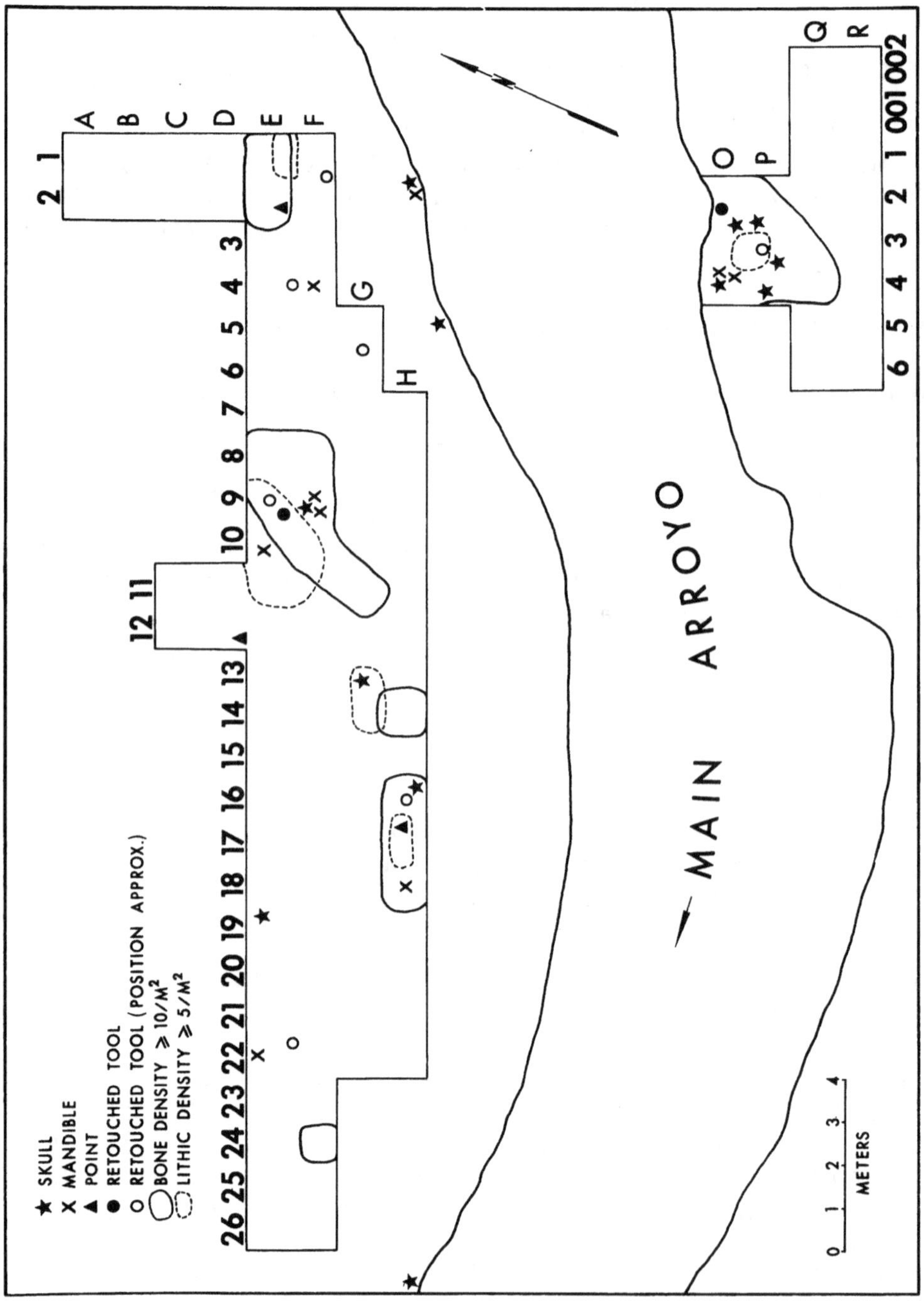

Fig. 9. Spatial distribution of bison remains and artifacts, showing clusters.

4. STRATIGRAPHY

The dates were run on specimens from the south side of the arroyo. The results probably reflect the chronological situation on the north side as well, but, because of the obvious problems of correlating between alluvial deposits on opposite sides of the arroyo, the dates should be applied to the north with caution.

The dates on samples P-2/27 and P-3/55 are entirely consistent with the stratigraphy, and suggest that the most intensive period of bison procurement probably occurred during the 15th or early 16th century. Earlier and later kill events are indicated, however, by the presence of bison bones, many showing clear signs of butchering, throughout most of the sequence exposed in the walls of the arroyo. These earlier and later kills will be investigated in forthcoming fieldwork.

Below the gravel beds containing the bison remains and artifacts, at a depth of about 1.8 m is a distinctive, 10- to 20-cm thick, greenish-grey soil horizon (Paleosol No. 2). A younger soil, referred to as Paleosol No. 1, is exposed in the arroyo walls farther upstream (see discussion below). Paleosol No. 2 probably reflects a period of widespread wet-meadow or marsh conditions in the wash (William R. Farrand, personal communication). This bed may be traced with little difficulty for at least 75 to 100 m upstream from the area of the 1977 excavations. Downstream, the paleosol is more difficult to follow. The majority of bison bones occur above this horizon. The age of the paleosol and the amount of time it represents are not known.

Below the paleosol for the next 80 cm, the sediments consist of several distinct beds of reddish-brown to brown coarse sands and gravels, frequently graded, and commonly containing large, angular blocks of gypsum up to 50 cm in diameter. Bison remains are present but rare in these deposits.

At a depth of approximately 2.7 m below the surface of the wash, another paleosol (No. 3) may be clearly recognized. This horizon is about 35 cm thick and consists of two parts. The basal 20 cm is a greenish-grey paleosol very similar to the one observed immediately beneath the gravels (No. 2). The lower part grades upward into a dark brownish-grey silt to medium sand with very distinctive vertical, blocky joints. The paleoenvironmental significance of this transition is unclear.

Below Paleosol No. 3, the deposits become sandier and lighter in color (light brown to yellowish-brown). The lowest meter of the sequence is obscured by a surficial layer of mudcracked silt, indicating that during flooding up to a meter of water may be ponded temporarily in the arroyo.

A third, very distinctive greenish-grey paleosol (No. 1) becomes visible in the arroyo walls about 60 to 80 m upstream from the 1977 excavations. This prominent horizon generally is over 20 cm thick and in places approaches 40 cm. This paleosol occurs about a meter below the rim of the arroyo and 50 to 80 cm above Paleosol No. 2. The sediments above the upper soil horizon are relatively fine, light reddish-brown silts and sands and contain almost no bison bones. The sediments between the two paleosols (Nos. 1 and 2) are somewhat darker, much coarser and contain frequent remains of bison. The upper paleosol has not been identified in the excavated area. A dark brown to black, possibly correlative, soil is exposed in the arroyo downstream from the site near the mouth of East Dimmitt Wash (William R. Farrand, personal communication).

In summary, there appear to be at least three distinct paleosols in the Garnsey Wash. Each of these horizons is overlain by beds of relatively coarse and poorly sorted alluvium. Bison were most intensively hunted in the wash during the period of alluviation following the formation of the second or middle paleosol. Limited radiocarbon evidence indicates that these procurement activities occurred during the 15th or early 16th century. Somewhat earlier and later kill events also occurred, at least intermittently, in the Garnsey Wash; the dating of these events remains to be established.

The three paleosols may represent periods, perhaps brief, when year-round moist conditions persisted over large parts of the wash. There is no evidence as yet to show that these soils have more than local environmental significance. Fluctuations in the amount of moisture in the wash may be linked to local changes in the karstic terrain. The possibility, of course, exists that one or more of these soils do, in fact, reflect regional climatic conditions. These prominent horizons will be investigated in considerably greater detail in forthcoming fieldwork.

5. THE BISON

Inventory

A total of 2231 complete and fragmentary bones were recovered from the Garnsey site in 1977. These bones are tabulated in Appendix I, and are accompanied by descriptive comments and measurements where appropriate. A key to the various symbols used in these tables also is provided. Of these bones, only three are non-bison (1 lumbar, 1 scapula, 1 radius). Although these three specimens have been included in the appendix, they have not as yet been identified to genus or species. A few additional non-bison remains have been omitted entirely from the tabulations in this report, because they too have not been identified. These include a number of rodent bones and several postcranial elements of a probable canid.

Of the 2228 bison bones, 1063 (47.7%) complete and fragmentary specimens were identifiable to specific skeletal part, an additional 583 (26.2%) represent small fragments of ribs or vertebral processes and 582 (26.1%) are unidentifiable debris. Table 2 provides an inventory by skeletal element of these remains. This table should not be used to estimate minimum number of individuals, however, because several of the fragments listed for a particular skeletal element may derive from the same bone. Minimum number of individuals is treated separately in Table 3.

Condition and Treatment

The bones from the Garnsey site generally are in good to excellent condition. In several instances preservation is remarkable. A few of the scapulae, for example, still preserve portions of cartilage on their proximal extremities. In addition, costal cartilage and sternebrae are well preserved. Some specimens at approximately the same depth, however, are badly weathered and corroded. This is especially true of material from Units Q and R on the south side of the arroyo. Other specimens are slightly abraded, although only a few, very small fragments actually qualify as waterworn. The weathering and abrasion of some of the bones may be the result of exposure on the surface of the wash prior to burial. They also may be the product of post-depositional soil-forming processes. The most poorly preserved bones, as might be expected, are those that were partially or completely exposed in the walls of the arroyo. These are bleached white, and many are cracked and very brittle.

Most specimens required no treatment prior to removal. When permitted to dry out slowly, they became relatively hard and stable. Initially, we made liberal use of acetone to dry the bones and dilute Elmer's glue to strengthen them. It became apparent that in most cases such treatment was unnecessary. The only items that required extensive treatment both in the field and in the laboratory were the skulls. They were thoroughly doused in the field with Elmer's glue and have been stabilized subsequently with a nonacetone- and nonwater-based lacquer ("Egyptian Cement"), recommended by the Museum of Paleontology at the University of Michigan. Specimens submitted for radiocarbon dating were left untreated. They were wrapped immediately in several

5. THE BISON

Table 2. Inventory of bison remains (complete and fragmentary) from the Garnsey site (1977).

Element	No.	%	Element (cont.)	No.	%
1. Skull	28	1.3	25. Radial Carpal	9	0.4
2. Mandible	9	0.4	26. Intermediate Carpal	12	0.5
3. Hyoid	8	0.4	27. Ulnar Carpal	9	0.4
4. Misc. Loose Teeth			28. Accessary Carpal	9	0.4
(Incisor/Canine)	17	0.8	29. Fused 2nd-3rd Carpal	8	0.4
5. Misc. Loose Teeth			30. 4th Carpal	10	0.4
(Molar/Premolar)	20	0.9	31. 5th Metacarpal	7	0.3
6. Misc. Tooth Frags.	101	4.5	32. Metacarpal	15	0.7
7. Atlas	12	0.5	33. Pelvis	25	1.1
8. Axis	8	0.4	34. Femur	14	0.6
9. Cervical (3-7)	36	1.6	35. Patella	5	0.2
10. Thoracic	75	3.4	36. Tibia	14	0.6
11. Lumbar	33	1.5	37. Astragalus	7	0.3
12. Sacrum	2	0.1	38. Lateral Malleolus	9	0.4
13. Caudal	18	0.8	39. Calcaneus	11	0.5
14. Unident. Vert. Body	11	0.5	40. Naviculo-Cuboid	10	0.4
15. Unident. Vert. Pad	43	1.9	41. 1st Tarsal	2	0.1
16. Unfused Vert. Summit	12	0.5	42. Fused 2nd-3rd Tarsal	4	0.2
17. Rib	85	3.8	43. 2nd Metatarsal	1	0.1
18. Misc. Rib-Vert.			44. Metatarsal	10	0.4
Process Frags.	583	26.2	45. Metapodial	2	0.1
19. Costal Cartilage	51	2.3	46. 1st Phalanx	47	2.1
20. Sternebra	19	0.9	47. 2nd Phalanx	35	1.6
21. Scapula	44	2.0	48. 3rd Phalanx	41	1.8
22. Humerus	15	0.7	49. Proximal Sesamoid	52	2.3
23. Radius	13	0.6	50. Distal Sesamoid	21	0.9
24. Ulna	14	0.6	51. Unident. Bone Frags.	582	26.1
			TOTAL	2228	99.9

layers of aluminum foil and placed in labeled double plastic bags. One specimen (0-4/13), in close proximity to a skull, apparently became contaminated with Elmer's glue and produced an aberrant date (see Table 1 above).

Minimum Number of Individuals

The minimum number of individuals (MNI) has been determined by dividing the number of each specific element recovered archaeologically by the number of that element in the animal. The results are tabulated in Table 3. The MNI are provided for each side of the arroyo separately, and for the site as a whole. The values for many of the elements presented in the table undoubtedly are conservative. For example, only proximal fragments of humeri, radii and ulnae have been used in the counts. Distal fragments have been excluded to avoid counting specimens that derive from the same bone. The decision as to which part of an element to use, of course, is arbitrary; distal fragments could have been used instead.

The values given in Table 3 are biased in favor of skulls (a total of 15 individuals, including 3 immature animals). A concerted effort was made to salvage skulls that were eroding from the walls of the arroyo. Three of these skulls ("BLM," CC-0035/1, F-0024/1) were found more than 20 m upstream from the 1977 excavations. Postcranial elements associated with these skulls were removed only if they too were in imminent danger of being destroyed by erosion or vandalism. Three other skulls (H-2/1, I-5/1, H-27/1), though found considerably closer to the main excavations, undoubtedly also contribute to some extent to the bias, again because associated postcranial elements were not removed. The areas from which skulls were salvaged will be investigated thoroughly in forthcoming excavations, eliminating much of the bias in the present MNI table.

The actual number of individuals represented in the 1977 materials is at least 17, including a minimum of 4 immature animals. In addition to the 12 mature and 3 immature crania, there are 2 mandibles with no age counterparts among the skulls (a neonatal individual and a three- to four-year old). The number of individuals just within the immediate area of the 1977 excavations (i.e., excluding the "BLM," CC-0035 and F-0024 specimens but including the two mandibles mentioned above) is 14, including 4 immature animals. The spatial distribution of these skulls and mandibles may be seen in Fig. 9.

Using 14 as the most reasonable estimate for the number of bison within the excavated areas and excluding all cranial and postcranial materials from the three upstream localities, it is possible to gain an impression of the degree to which each skeletal element deviates from the number to be expected if no parts were lost or removed from the site (Fig. 10). This figure must be regarded as extremely preliminary; it will almost certainly change in the future as the sample is enlarged and as a statistically less biased sampling procedure is introduced.

Age and Sex

Several different criteria have been used to age the Garnsey site cranial material: (1) eruption and wear sequence of the lower and upper dentitions (Frison et al. 1976, 1978; Reher 1974; Wilson 1974); (2) degree of fusion of the parietofrontal and frontal sutures (Shackleton et al. 1975); (3) degree of rugosity of the basal horn-core burr and orbital rim in males (Shackleton et al. 1975; Skinner and Kaisen 1947). The second and third criteria were useful, particularly in males, to distinguish between mature and immature specimens when the dentitions were missing. The data on age are included in the appropriate tables in Appendix I.

The age estimates presented in this report probably may be made more precise, perhaps to the point of indicating the season of death. This has not been attempted in the present study, however, because adequate comparative materials were not at hand. Moreover, the rate of dental attrition in the

Table 3. [a]Minimum number of individuals (MNI)

Element		[b]North No.	North MNI	[c]South No.	South MNI	[d]Combined No.	Combined MNI
1. Skull:	-	[e]7(1)	7(1)	8(2)	8(2)	15(3)	15(3)
2. Mandible:	L	4(1)	4(1)	1	1	5(1)	5(1)
	R	3	3	1	1	4	4
3. Hyoid:	L	3(1)	3(1)	0	0	3(1)	3(1)
	R	4	4	0	0	4	[f]5(1)
4. Atlas:	-	3	3	9	9	12	12
5. Axis:	-	4(1)	4(1)	4	4	8(1)	8(1)
6. [g]Cervical:	-	15(1)	3(1)	11	3	26(1)	6(1)
7. [g]Thoracic:	-	29(2)	3(1)	23(1)	2(1)	52(3)	[h]5(2)
8. [g]Lumbar:	-	11	3	11	3	22	[h]6
9. Sacrum:	-	2	2	0	0	2	2
10. [g]Caudal:	-	14	1	3	1	17	1
11. Rib:	L	28(3)	2(1)	7(1)	1(1)	35(4)	[h]3(2)
	R	40(4)	3(1)	7(2)	1(1)	47(6)	[h]4(2)
12. Costal Cartilage:	-	42	2	9	1	51	[h]3
13. Sternebra:	-	15	3	4	1	19	[h]4
14. [i]Scapula:	L	5	5	0	0	5	5
	R	1	1	2	2	3	3
15. [j]Humerus:	L	1	1	4(2)	4(2)	5(2)	5(2)
	R	4(1)	4(1)	4(2)	4(2)	8(3)	8(3)
16. [j]Radius:	L	2	2	1	1	3	3
	R	4(1)	4(1)	3(2)	3(2)	7(3)	7(3)
17. [j]Ulna:	L	4(1)	4(1)	0	0	4(1)	4(1)
	R	4(1)	4(1)	2	2	6(1)	6(1)
18. Radial Carpal:	L	3	3	1	1	4	4
	R	3	3	2	2	5	5
19. Intermed. Carpal:	L	5	5	0	0	5	5
	R	5	5	2	2	7	7
20. Ulnar Carpal:	L	3	3	2	2	5	5
	R	3	3	1	1	4	4
21. Accessary Carpal:	L	4	4	2	2	6	6
	R	3	3	0	0	3	3

Table 3. (cont.)

Element		[b]North No.	North MNI	[c]South No.	South MNI	[d]Combined No.	Combined MNI
22. Fused 2nd and 3rd Carpal:	L	2	2	2	2	4	4
	R	2	2	2	2	4	4
23. 4th Carpal:	L	3	3	2	2	5	5
	R	3	3	1	1	4	4
24. 5th Metacarpal:	-	2	1	5	3	7	4
25. [j]Metacarpal:	L	4(2)	4(2)	2	2	6(2)	6(2)
	R	4(1)	4(1)	2	2	6(1)	6(1)
26. [k]Pelvis:	L	2	2	1	1	3	3
	R	6	6	3(1)	3(1)	9(1)	9(1)
27. [j]Femur:	L	1	1	1	1	2	2
	R	4	4	1(1)	1(1)	5(1)	5(1)
28. Patella:	L	1	1	1	1	2	2
	R	2	2	1	1	3	3
29. [j]Tibia:	L	6(1)	6(1)	0	0	6(1)	6(1)
	R	1	1	5(3)	5(3)	6(3)	6(3)
30. Astragalus:	L	4	4	1	1	5	5
	R	1	1	1	1	2	2
31. Lateral Malleolus:	L	6	6	0	0	6	6
	R	3	3	0	0	3	3
32. Calcaneus:	L	3	3	2	2	5	5
	R	5(1)	5(1)	1(1)	1(1)	6(2)	6(2)
33. Naviculo-Cuboid:	L	5	5	0	0	5	5
	R	5	5	0	0	5	5
34. 1st Tarsal:	L	0	0	0	0	0	0
	R	1	1	0	0	1	1
35. Fused 2nd and 3rd Tarsal:	L	1	1	0	0	1	1
	R	3	3	0	0	3	3
36. 2nd Metatarsal:	-	1	1	0	0	1	1
37. [j]Metatarsal:	L	5	5	1	1	6	[f]7(1)
	R	3	3	1(1)	1(1)	4(1)	4(1)
38. 1st Phalanx:	"L"	14	4	4(1)	1(1)	18(1)	5(1)
	"R"	17(1)	5(1)	7	2	24(1)	[h]7(1)

Table 3. (cont.)

Element		[b]North No.	North MNI	[c]South No.	South MNI	[d]Combined No.	Combined MNI
39. 2nd Phalanx:	"L"	13(1)	4(1)	6	2	19(1)	[f]7(2)
	"R"	13(1)	4(1)	3(1)	1(1)	16(2)	5(2)
40. 3rd Phalanx:	"L"	12	3	5	2	17	5
	"R"	13(1)	4(1)	11	3	24(1)	6(1)
41. Proximal Sesamoid:	"L",C	7	2	3	1	10	3
	"L",P	9	3	10	3	19	[h]6
	"R",C	10	3	3	1	13	4
	"R",P	8	2	2	1	10	3
42. Distal Sesamoid:	"L"	9	3	2	1	11	[h]4
	"R"	9	3	1	1	10	[h]4

[a]MNI (Minimum Number of Individuals); bison only; determined by dividing number of each specific element recovered archaeologically by number of that element in animal.

[b]North side of arroyo (Units A, B, C, D, E, F, G, H, I).

[c]South side of arroyo (Units CC, FF, O, P, Q, R).

[d]North and South sides of arroyo combined.

[e]Numbers in parentheses refer to number of immature elements and minimum number of immature individuals.

[f]Figure includes adjustment for number of immature individuals.

[g]Includes only specimens in which at least part of vertebral body is preserved.

[h]In most cases, the combined MNI obtained by dividing the combined or total number of an element for the site as a whole by the number of that element in the animal is identical to the figure obtained by adding the separate MNIs for the North and South sides of the arroyo; the latter figure is used in those cases in which it is higher.

[i]Includes only specimens in which at least part of glenoid cavity and neck are preserved.

[j]Includes only specimens in which at least part of proximal end is preserved.

[k]Includes only specimens in which at least part of acetabulum is preserved.

5. THE BISON

	[a]OE	[b]EE	[c]PCT
SKULL	12	14	85.7
ATLAS	11	14	78.6
AXIS	8	14	57.1
HUMERUS	13	28	46.4
INTERMEDIATE CARPAL	12	28	42.9
METACARPAL	12	28	42.9
PELVIS	11	28	39.3
CALCANEUS	11	28	39.3
1ST PHALANX	42	112	37.5
CERVICAL (3-7)	26	70	37.1
3RD PHALANX	41	112	36.6
TIBIA	10	28	35.7
NAVICULO-CUBOID	10	28	35.7
METATARSAL	10	28	35.7
MANDIBLE	9	28	32.1
RADIUS	9	28	32.1
ULNA	9	28	32.1
RADIAL CARPAL	9	28	32.1
ULNAR CARPAL	9	28	32.1
ACCESSORY CARPAL	9	28	32.1
4TH CARPAL	9	28	32.1
LATERAL MALLEOLUS	9	28	32.1
2ND PHALANX	35	112	31.3
LUMBAR	21	70	30.0
FUSED 2ND-3RD CARPAL	8	28	28.6
THORACIC	52	196	26.5
HYOID	7	28	25.0
SCAPULA	7	28	25.0
5TH METACARPAL	7	28	25.0
FEMUR	7	28	25.0
ASTRAGALUS	7	28	25.0
PROXIMAL SESAMOID	52	224	23.2
RIB	80	392	20.4
STERNEBRA	19	98	19.4
DISTAL SESAMOID	21	112	18.8
PATELLA	5	28	17.9
SACRUM	2	14	14.3
FUSED 2ND-3RD TARSAL	4	28	14.3
COSTAL CARTILAGE	51	392	13.0
CAUDAL	17	280	6.1
1ST TARSAL	1	28	3.6
2ND METATARSAL	1	28	3.6

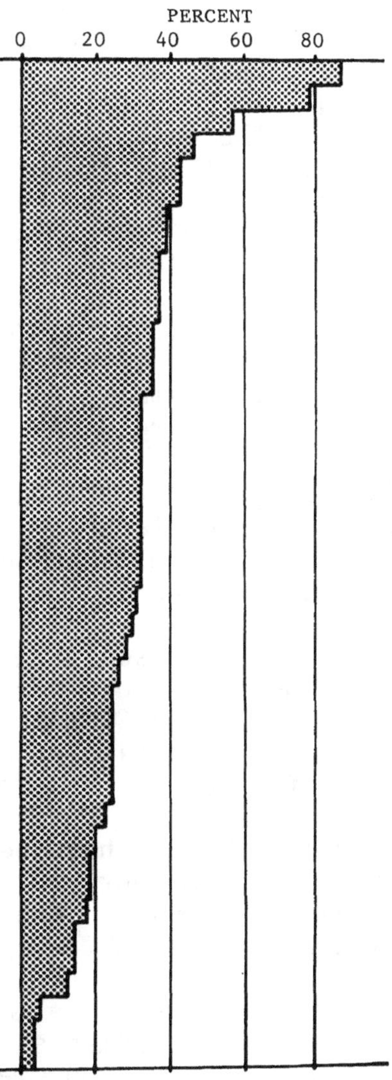

[a]Observed number of elements.

[b]Expected number of elements.

[c]Percent.

Fig. 10. Observed versus expected number of skeletal elements.

Southern Plains may differ somewhat from that in the Northern Plains. Until such differences are clearly worked out with modern materials, it is safer not to be overly precise in estimating the ages of the Garnsey bison.

Of the 17 individuals recovered from the Garnsey site (15 skulls plus 2 mandibles with no age counterparts among the skulls), 4 (23.5%) are immature (less than three years of age) and 13 (76.5%) are mature. Within the immature group, 1 (25.0%) is neonatal and 3 (75.0%) are between the ages of one and two years. All 3 of the latter differ slightly from each other in age. Within the mature group, 3 (23.1%) could not be aged precisely. Of these, at least 2 are relatively old. Of the remaining mature animals, 1 (7.7%) is between three and four years of age. The others (69.2%) are all older than six years of age, and most are older than eight.

In summary, the bison recovered from the Garnsey site during the 1977 field season consist of several immature animals and a greater number of fully mature to old animals. Prime adults in the range between three and six or seven years of age are underrepresented.

The degree of epiphyseal fusion of postcranial elements is also tabulated in Appendix I. Three states have been recorded: (1) unfused; (2) fusing; (3) fused. These data have not as yet been analyzed, but they are readily accessible in the tables.

The sex of the Garnsey cranial material was most readily determined with the transverse horn-core diameters and the cranial widths (Measurements 12 and 14, respectively, of Skinner and Kaisen 1947). In addition, the mandibles were sexed using the mandibular widths below M3 as described by Reher (1974). The relevant data are provided in Appendix I.

The 12 mature crania have been sexed; 6 are males and 6 are females. In addition, the three-to four-year old mandible, which has no age equivalent among the skulls, is male. Thus the sex ratio of the present sample is nearly 50:50, deviating very slightly in favor of males.

Many of the postcranial elements (e.g., metatarsals and metacarpals) also may be sexed using measurements provided in Appendix I (cf. Bedord 1974). The samples presently are too small, however, to be reliable. Sexing of the postcranial material, therefore, will be deferred for the future.

Butchering

A formal analysis of the butchering evidence at the Garnsey site has not been completed. Nevertheless, certain observations may be made that will be useful in comparisons of the Garnsey material with butchered remains from other sites.

Perhaps the most striking aspect of the Garnsey evidence is its similarity to the butchering patterns described by Frison et al. (1976) at the Hawken site, a much earlier bison kill in eastern Wyoming. Many of the skeletal elements at

5. THE BISON

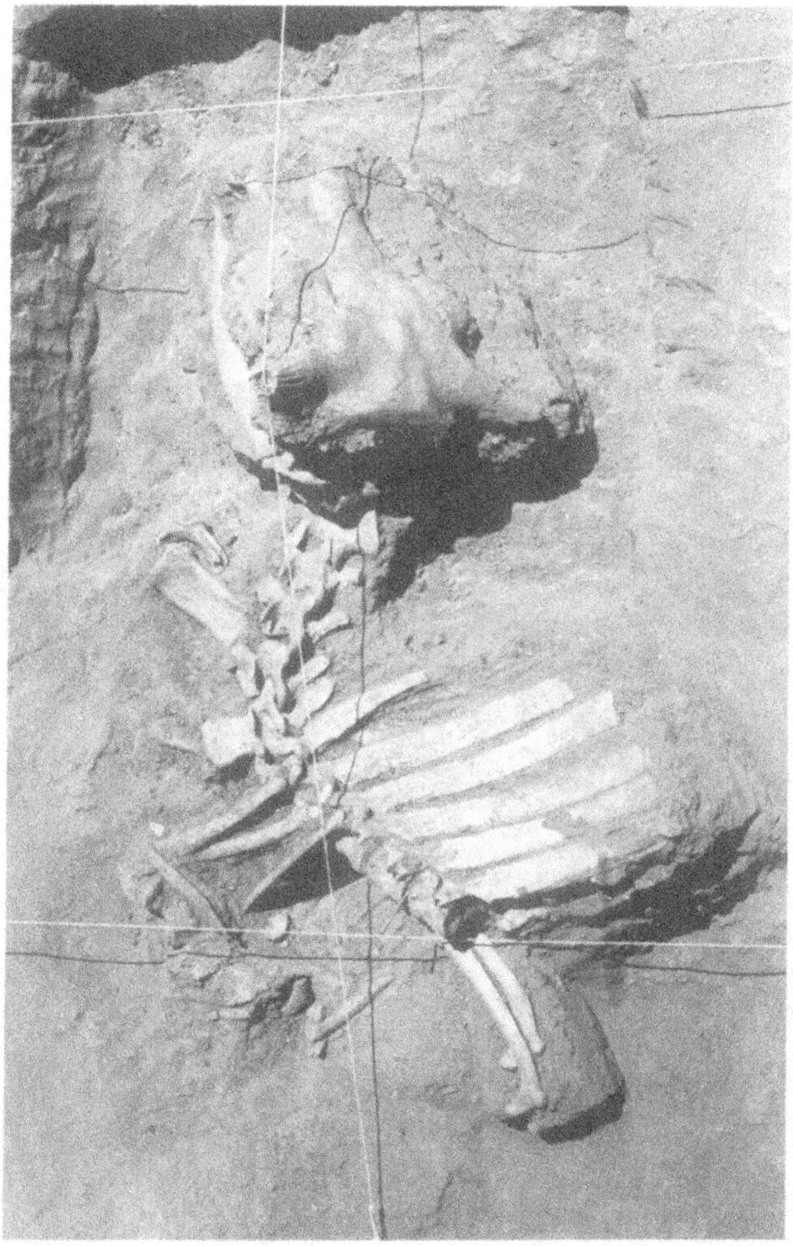

Fig. 11. Articulated front-end of bison in Units EF-9, 10.

the two sites have been treated in almost identical fashion. Perhaps the single most obvious difference between the two is the scarcity of cut-marks on bone surfaces at the Garnsey site. Their infrequent occurrence, however, may be more the result of post-depositional weathering and abrasion than of real differences in overall butchering practices.

Skulls generally were separated from the vertebral column. The only exception was a completely articulated front-end found in Units EF-9,10 (Fig. 11), consisting of the skull (F-9/28), cervicals, five thoracics with associated ribs, and both front legs. Skulls and mandibles seldom showed direct evidence of butchering. Horn-cores, frontals, nasals, occipitals, ascending rami and so forth generally were left intact. The teeth in one mandible and in one unrelated maxilla, however, were smashed almost to the level of the alveoli.

Cervicals and thoracics generally were left intact. The transverse and vertical processes in the lumbars, however, often were broken off (Fig. 12). The presence of several isolated, broken vertebral bodies indicates that some vertebrae were completely demolished during the butchering process. Only two sacra were found; one of these had been cleaved off near the cranial end.

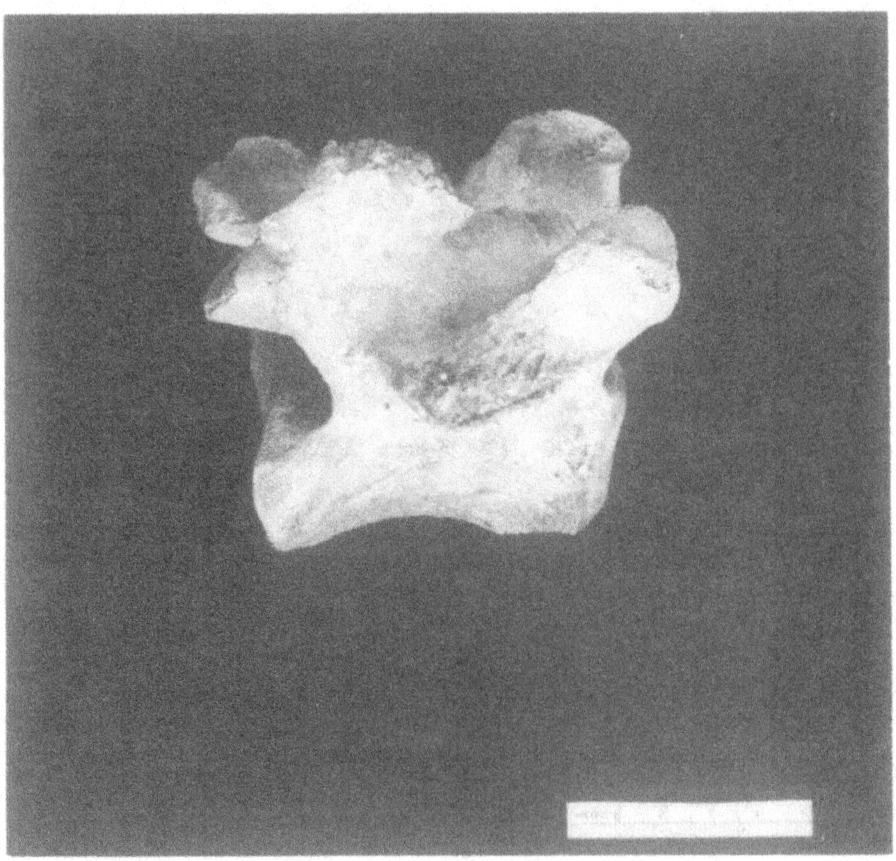

Fig. 12. Butchered lumbar vertebra.

Ribs are perhaps the most thoroughly butchered skeletal element at the Garnsey site. The shafts commonly were broken just below their proximal ends (Fig. 13, center left and center right of figure). Many of the shafts subsequently were comminuted with cleaver-like blows into tiny fragments and splinters.

Blades, caudal blade borders and spines of scapulae frequently were broken off (Fig. 13, extreme left and extreme right of figure). The shafts of humeri were broken just proximal of the midpoint, often near the deltoid tuberosity. The olecranon, in several cases, was broken from the ulna and often the entire proximal end of the ulna was broken from its shaft (the latter breakage may be a post-depositional phenomenon). The shafts of radii were broken obliquely, often forming pointed fragments that may have been used as chopping tools. An example is illustrated in Figure 14. Metacarpals generally were left intact.

The pelves were heavily butchered at the Garnsey site. Usually they were taken apart at or near the narrowest points (i.e., at the pubis and ischiatic notches). A commonly encountered fragment consisted of little more than the acetabulum with small portions of the ilium and ischium (Fig. 15). Femurs were broken near the midpoint of the shaft, and occasionally the trochanter major and trochlea were chopped off. Tibia shafts also were broken, and several butchered specimens may have functioned as chopping tools. The distal anterior process of one calcaneus had been chopped off by a sharp, cleaver-like blow. Metatarsals, like metacarpals, showed no clear evidence of butchering.

Method of Procurement

The method of bison procurement employed at the Garnsey site is not clearly understood at present. Resolution of this critical problem depends on obtaining much more detailed information on the chronology and stratigraphy of the site, particularly the microstratigraphic relationships among bone clusters within the channel deposits. Also needed is a much clearer picture of the paleoenvironment of the wash and surrounding areas, in order to understand the factors which attracted bison to the wash. A larger, and statistically more reliable sample of the bison population also would help to identify the method of procurement.

It is perhaps easiest and safest at this preliminary stage of the investigations to rule out certain methods. For example, the site is unlikely to have been a jump. The bedrock walls of the wash, at least today, are neither high enough nor steep enough. Modern domestic cattle go freely in and out of the wash almost anywhere along its course. Nor does the wash terminate today in an effective box canyon. Instead, it becomes progressively shallower as one moves upstream until it ultimately grades into the surrounding terrain. It must be stressed, however, that the bedrock is extremely soft and unstable, and subject to considerable karstic activity. It is conceivable, though rather unlikely, that the configuration of the wash has changed dramatically over the past several centuries.

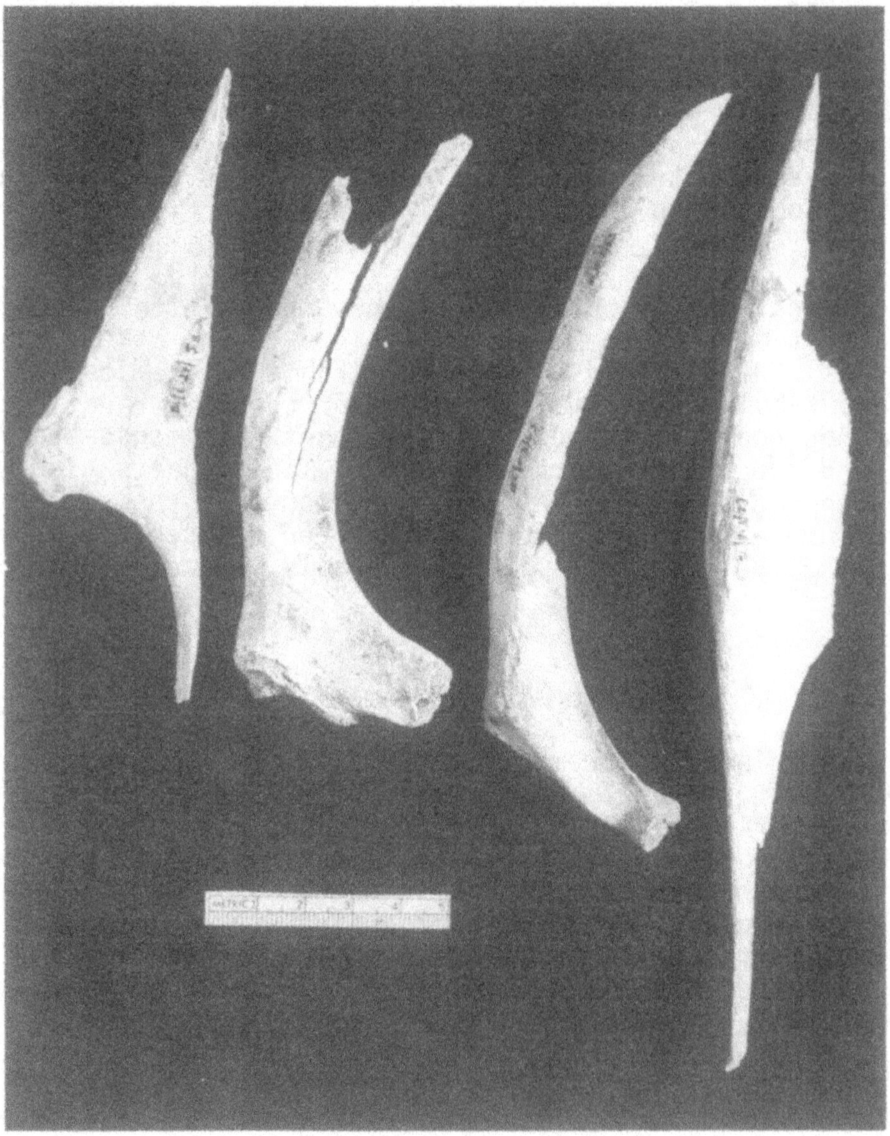

Fig. 13. Proximal ends of butchered ribs (center left and center right); spines of butchered scapulae (extreme left and extreme right).

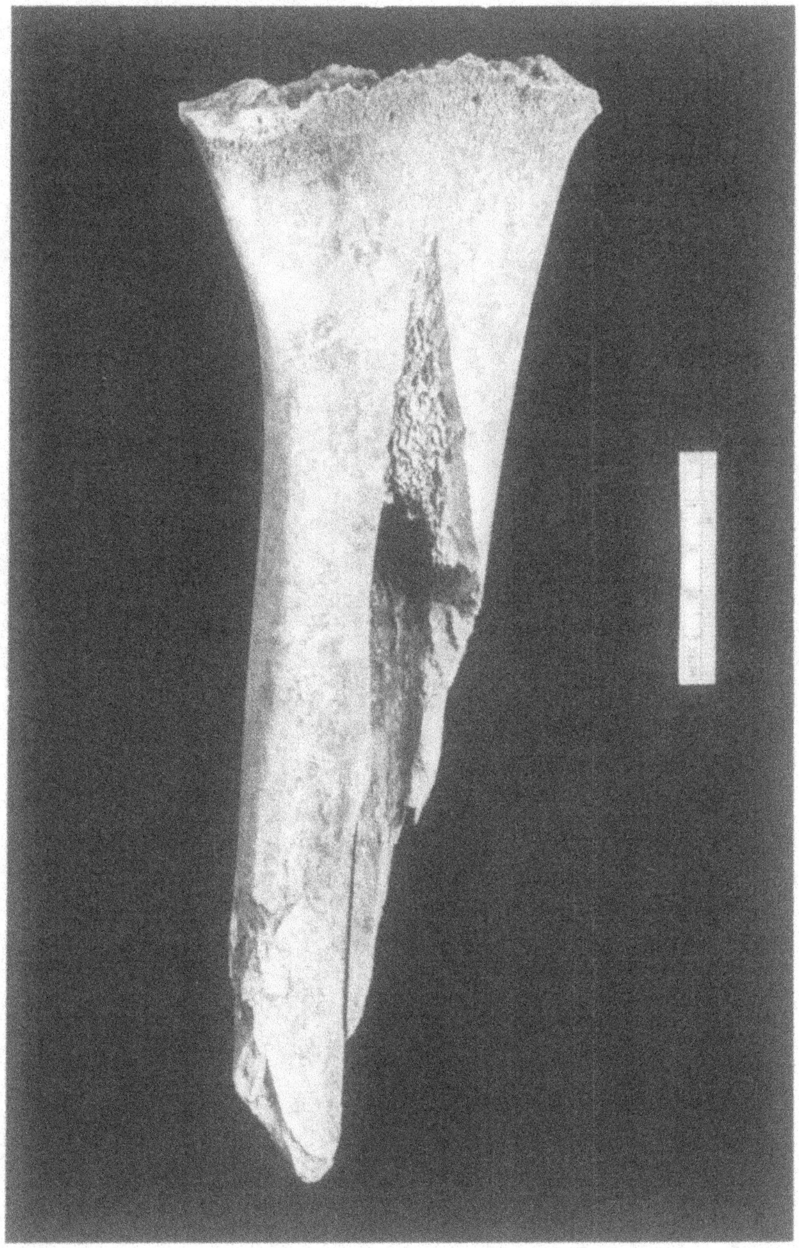

Fig. 14. Butchered radius.

5. THE BISON

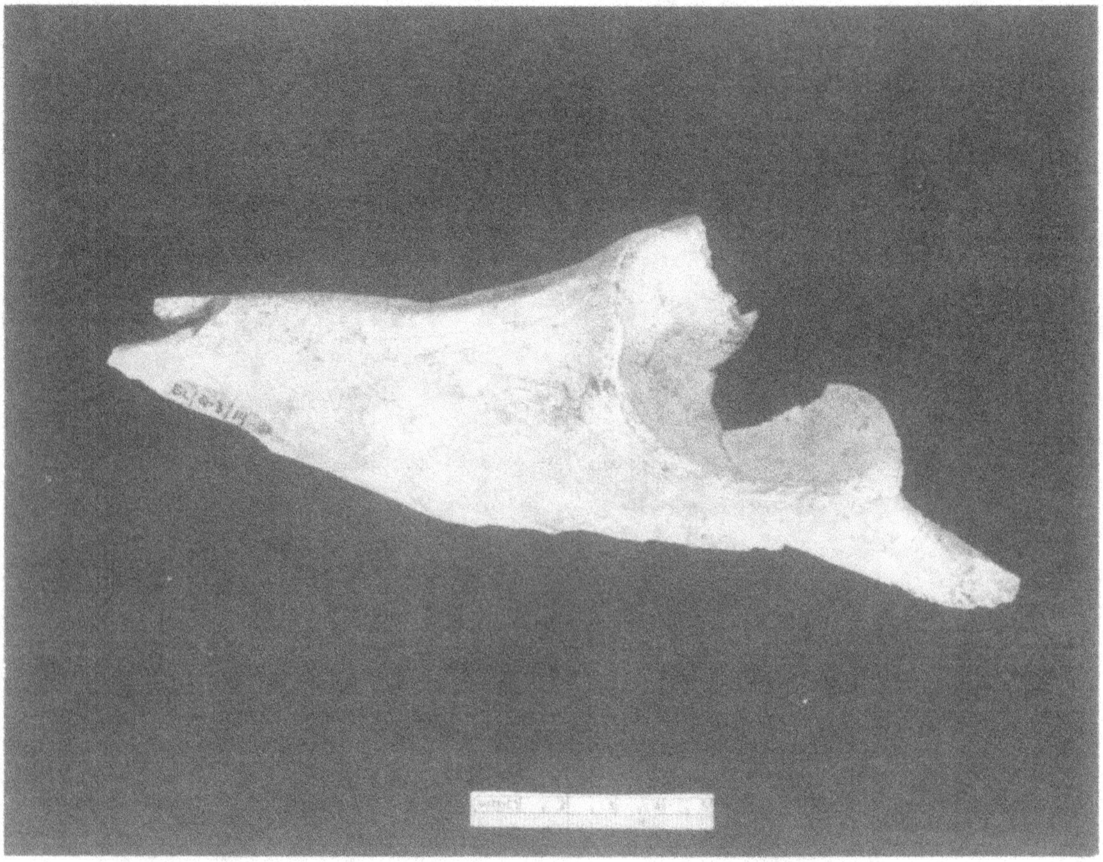

Fig. 15. Butchered fragment of pelvis.

Bison may have been contained or trapped by some form of surround or rudimentary corral. Unfortunately, at this point there is very little direct evidence to support or refute the use of either of these forms of entrapment.

Periodic ambush of animals grazing in the wash is perhaps the method that best fits the data available at present. It would account for the generally low density of bone at the site, the spatial distribution of bone in distinct, isolated clusters, and the association of bone with more than a single bed within and adjacent to the channels. Periodic ambush also might account for the predominance of older, and presumably more vulnerable animals at the Garnsey site. These conclusions, however, must be regarded as extremely tentative until more of the site has been sampled and until much more is known concerning the depositional history and paleoenvironmental setting of the site.

6. LITHIC ARTIFACTS AND CERAMICS

General Description of the Assemblage

A total of 149 artifacts (excluding possible bone tools) were recovered from the Garnsey site during the 1977 field season. These include 3 projectile points, 2 other bifaces, 1 core, 6 ceramic body sherds and 137 unifacial lithic artifacts. The unifacial artifacts consist almost exclusively of small unmodified flakes, probably the products of tool utilization and resharpening. This assemblage apparently reflects a limited range of activities relating to the procurement and inital processing of bison.

Distribution of the Artifacts

Artifacts were distributed non-randomly throughout the areas of the site excavated in 1977. In general, the distribution of artifacts closely corresponded to the distribution of bison bone. Where bone was rare or absent, artifacts also were rare or absent; where bone was present in significant quantity, artifacts also were relatively numerous. Interestingly, artifact density tended to be highest at the margins of the bone concentrations. On the average, artifact density was low (1.2 items per m^2). The spatial distribution of artifacts and the relationship of artifacts to bone clusters are illustrated in Figure 9.

The majority of artifacts, like bison bones, were recovered from the gravels in and adjacent to the channels in the alluvium overlying Paleosol No. 2. Although many of the artifacts were broken, few if any show macroscopic damage (such as polishing or crushing) resulting from transport. If transport of the artifacts has occurred, it has taken place over short distances only. This observation, together with the close correspondence of the distributions of artifacts and bison bones, suggests that the artifacts are in fact associated with the bison remains.

Condition of the Lithic Artifacts

A large proportion of the lithic artifacts are in fragmentary condition. Only 39.2% (56 of 143) appear to be essentially intact. The remainder are broken, with 32.9% (47 of 143) showing two or more probable breaks. This extensive damage was not the result of transport or of other depositional or post-depositional geologic processes (William R. Farrand, personal communication). It is possible that this damage may be the result of heat stress, reflecting aboriginal use of fire at the site. Clear macroscopic fire damage (potlid fractures and/or lateral shattering) was observed on 14.0% (20 of 143) of the specimens. In addition, many others showed discoloration of unbroken surfaces, possibly due to exposure to heat. It is not known at present whether the heating or burning of the specimens was intentional or accidental. Moreover, it should be noted that to date no hearths or firepits have been encountered at the Garnsey site.

6. LITHIC ARTIFACTS AND CERAMICS

Description of the Ceramic Artifacts

A total of six undecorated body sherds were recovered from the Garnsey site. These may be divided into two types:

(1) Light tan paste, very fine grit temper; surface polished, black; thickness undetermined; represented by a single small, foliated fragment; weight 0.23 g.

(2) Reddish-brown paste with brown to black core, fine to medium grit temper (grains up to 1 mm); surfaces unevenly smoothed, brown with some blackened areas; thickness ranges from 4.5 to 5.5 mm; represented by five small sherds; total weight 3.50 g, range of individual weights 0.29 to 1.01 g; similar to "Jornada Brown" as described by Runyan and Hedrick (1973).

Description of the Lithic Artifacts

Lithic Material: A range of different materials were employed in the manufacture of artifacts. The majority were made from fine-grained chert or chalcedony, of which several varieties were recognized. Smaller quantities of quartzite, basalt, and obsidian were employed also. The frequency of each type of material within the total Garnsey site assemblage is summarized in Table 4. Locally available materials include mottled grey-tan-and-blue chert, grey chert, milky iron-stained chalcedony, and probably others. These are found in gravels in, or derived from, the Pliocene Ogallala Formation on the Llano Estacado (Kelley 1971). Similar cherts, particularly the greys and blues, may also be found in the Permian San Andres Formation west of Roswell. At least 50% of the artifacts, and probably more, are made from these locally obtained materials. A few of the materials are known to be non-local: the red-to-yellow chert probably comes from the Alibates quarries in the Texas Panhandle, while the obsidian and fingerprint chert probably originated from sources to the west. These non-local materials together comprise about 10% of the sample. The sources of the remaining materials have not been determined.

Projectile Points: Three projectile points were recovered from the Garnsey site during the 1977 field season. One is complete, and the other two are represented by distal fragments only (Fig. 16). All three points are made from grey-tan-and-blue mottled chert which probably was locally obtained.

The complete specimen (H-17/1) is a small, narrow triangular side-notched point with straight base and square tang. The blade is slightly beveled, and there are distinct fine serrations on both lateral edges of the blade and on the base.

One of the distal fragments (E-2/4) also represents a small, narrow triangular side-notched point with weak, fine serrations on both lateral edges of the blade. This specimen was broken at the notches, and the base is missing. The tip is also slightly damaged. The point was manufactured by retouching a flake, and some of the unmodified ventral surface of the flake remains.

6. LITHIC ARTIFACTS AND CERAMICS

Table 4. Lithic materials utilized at the Garnsey site

Type	No.	%
1. Mottled, and/or banded, grey-tan-and-blue chert	55	38.5
2. Grey chert	13	9.1
3. Chalky white-to-tan chert	12	8.4
4. Milky, iron-stained chalcedony	9	6.3
5. Basalt (or similar fine-grained igneous rock)	8	5.6
6. Red-to-yellow mottled chert	7	4.9
7. Dark red-purple quartzite	6	4.2
8. Yellow-to-tan chalcedony	6	4.2
9. Grey chalcedony	5	3.5
10. Banded olive-brown-tan-and-grey chalcedony	5	3.5
11. Black mottled chert	4	2.8
12. Olive-green chert	4	2.8
13. Unidentified non-siliceous, weathered rock	3	2.1
14. Fingerprint chert	2	1.4
15. White chert	1	0.7
16. Grainy dark-brown chert	1	0.7
17. Grainy pink chalcedony	1	0.7
18. Obsidian	1	0.7
TOTAL	143	100.1

The other distal fragment (D-12/1) represents a larger, broader point, with distinct serrations on both lateral edges of the blade. This specimen is broken near the midpoint of the blade. The tip is damaged.

The three projectile points are described in detail in the following section. The descriptive terms used are those proposed and defined by Binford (1963).

A. Complete Projectile Point (H-17/1)

(1) Blade shape: triangular outline, biconvex transverse section, symmetrical.
(2) Longitudinal section of projectile: biplano.
(3) Blade chipping scars: primary scars diminutive, flat, lamellar, bifacially placed; secondary scars smooth, lamellar, continuous, and placed bilaterally on alternate faces; lateral edges of blade finely serrated, perhaps largely as a result of the technique of retouching.
(4) Base: straight, bifacially thinned, finely serrated, slightly projecting lateral "ears," grinding absent.
(5) Juncture: lateral-lateral juncture, with acute-angular distal point of juncture, acute medial points of juncture, and right-angled-angular proximal point of juncture.
(6) Haft element: symmetrical, grinding absent.
(7) Tang: parallel, grinding absent.

Fig. 16. Projectile points from the Garnsey site.

(8) Metric attributes:
   (a) Width of base (max.) 11.5 mm
   (b) Width at notches 4.5 mm
   (c) Width at shoulder 10.0 mm
   (d) Total axial length 27.5 mm
   (e) Blade length 20.5 mm
   (f) Notch length 2.0 mm
   (g) Thickness (max.) 2.5 mm
   (h) Weight 0.71 g

B. Distal Fragment of Projectile Point (E-2/4)

(1) Blade shape: excurvate-incurvate outline, plano-convex transverse section, symmetrical.

(2) Longitudinal section of projectile: asymmetrically concave-convex.

(3) Blade chipping scars: primary scars diminutive, flat, expanding, placed on external face only (internal face is the fracture face of the original flake blank); secondary scars expanding, discontinuous, and placed unifacially-bilaterally (on internal face); lateral

edges of blade finely serrated, perhaps largely as a result of the technique of retouching.

(4) Base: absent.
(5) Juncture: absent.
(6) Haft element: absent.
(7) Tang: absent.
(8) Metric attributes:
 (a) Width at shoulder 11.5 mm
 (b) Blade length (approx.) 26.0 mm
 (c) Thickness (max.) 3.0 mm
 (d) Weight 1.03 g

C. Distal Fragment of Projectile Point (D-12/1)
(1) Blade shape: biconvex transverse section, symmetrical.
(2) Longitudinal section of projectile: incomplete.
(3) Blade chipping scars: primary scars diminutive, flat, lamellar, bifacially placed; secondary scars smooth, lamellar, continuous, and placed bifacially; lateral edges of blade serrated.
(4) Base: absent.
(5) Juncture: absent.
(6) Haft element: absent.
(7) Tang: absent.
(8) Metric attributes:
 (a) Width at midpoint of blade 17.0 mm
 (b) Blade length greater than 16.0 mm
 (c) Thickness (max.) 4.0 mm
 (d) Weight 0.91 g

Bifaces and Core: Two bifaces and one core were recovered during the 1977 field season. One biface (E-9/16), chipped from a mottled green-grey basaltic material, is the fragmentary midsection of a narrow, thick blade (width 19.0 mm; thickness 8.0 mm; weight 2.74 g). The edges are battered and steep but do not appear to be utilized. This item probably represents an unfinished tool, possibly a point preform, broken during manufacture (Fig. 17).

The other biface (0-2/16) is complete. It is a thick, crudely chipped ovate biface, manufactured from a yellow-red mottled chert. Four sections of the lateral edge show damage or wear as the result of utilization, in the form of microretouch (edge angle 50°), and in the form of battering and scalar retouch (edge angle 75° to 80°). These two forms of retouch correspond approximately to types "g" and "e," respectively, as illustrated in Brézillon (1971: 109). The use damage suggests that this biface served as a tool, and may have been utilized for more than one function. Overall dimensions of the biface are: length 43.5 mm; width 36.0 mm; thickness 15.0 mm; weight 23.5 g (Fig. 17).

The core (E-7/S) is a small flat pebble (diameter 28.0 mm; weight 9.4 g) of light grey chert from which one large flake and several smaller ones were removed. No subsequent attempt was made to utilize the core (Fig. 17).

6. LITHIC ARTIFACTS AND CERAMICS

Fig. 17. Bifaces (left, E-9/16; right, O-2/16) and core (center, E-7/S) from Garnsey site (original lateral edge of specimen on left is toward top of photograph; note that scale is in inches).

Unifacial Artifacts: The unifacial artifacts consist primarily of small, unmodified retouch and resharpening flakes. Also included in this group are two complete endscrapers, several fragments of unifacially retouched tools and a number of utilized flakes. In the following discussion, all of the unifacial items, whether unmodified or modified, are first analyzed together as a group. Then additional data are presented for the modified pieces alone. Selection of attributes for these analyses was based largely on a list proposed by Wilmsen (1970), with minor revisions for the purposes of this study. The metric attributes include:

(1) Weight (grams)
(2) Length of medial axis (mm; on fragments where the medial axis could not be determined, maximum overall length was measured)
(3) Maximum width (mm; perpendicular to medial axis)
(4) Thickness at bulb of percussion (mm)
(5) Maximum thickness below bulb (mm)
(6) Medial axis angle (intersection, on ventral face, of medial axis with plane of striking platform)
(7) Platform angle (intersection of projected plane of platform with ventral face below bulb)
(8) Maximum width of platform (mm)
(9) Thickness of platform (mm; measured at cone on plane of platform)

6. LITHIC ARTIFACTS AND CERAMICS

The metric attributes recorded for the Garnsey assemblage are tabulated in Table 5. Skewness and kurtosis have been calculated for each of the attributes, according to the formulas provided in footnotes *a* and *b* of the table. Further discussion of these formulas may be found in Ferguson (1966:76). Frequency distributions for medial axis angles and platform angles are shown graphically in Figure 18 and Figure 19, respectively. Both attributes have unimodal and essentially normal distributions. Weight deviates substantially from a normal distribution. This is due primarily to the inclusion of a single, very large utilized flake (D-32/1). The majority of flakes weigh considerably less than a gram. Several of the other attributes listed in Table 5 also are skewed by the inclusion of D-32/1. In these cases, the median values most closely reflect the nature of the assemblage.

Table 5. Metric attributes of unifacial lithic artifacts

Attribute	No.	Min.	Max.	Med.	Mean	S	[a]Skew.	[b]Kurt.
Weight	136	0.01	48.33	0.24	0.92	4.19	10.79	119.31
Length	136	3.0	57.0	10.0	11.5	6.36	3.25	18.49
Width	136	3.0	37.0	9.5	10.7	5.04	1.75	5.39
Bulb Th.	75	0.5	13.5	2.5	2.9	2.07	2.03	7.36
Max. Th.	136	0.5	20.0	2.5	3.2	2.76	3.11	14.39
Med. Ax. Ang.	64	65	130	90	91	13.72	0.19	-0.01
Plat. Angle	62	10	135	70	73	23.91	0.37	0.74
Plat. Width	68	1.0	31.0	6.0	6.6	4.90	2.31	8.00
Plat. Th.	70	0.0	9.0	2.0	2.4	1.83	1.18	1.37
Len./Wid.	136	0.4	2.8	---	1.1	0.41	1.09	2.03
Len./Th.	136	1.1	20.0	---	5.0	3.03	2.15	6.73

[a]Skew (Skewness = $m_3/(m_2)^{3/2}$ where m_j is the jth sample moment).

[b]Kurt (Kurtosis = $(m_4/m_2^2)-3$ where m_j is the jth sample moment).

In addition to the metric attributes recorded for each unifacial artifact, several categorical attributes relating to the geometry of the specimen also were described. These are listed below.

(1) Maximum width position (measured on a scale from 1 to 5; where 1 = maximum width at platform, 3 = maximum width at midpoint of medial axis, 5 = maximum width at termination)

(2) Platform preparation (unmodified cortex, unmodified tool edge, flat, or faceted)

(3) Platform abrasion (present or absent)

(4) Termination (feathered or hinged)

(5) Dorsal face (unmodified cortex, cortex modified by some flaking, flat, flaked)

(6) Condition (complete, proximal fragment, distal fragment, medial or lateral fragment)

(7) Type (unmodified, utilized, retouched)

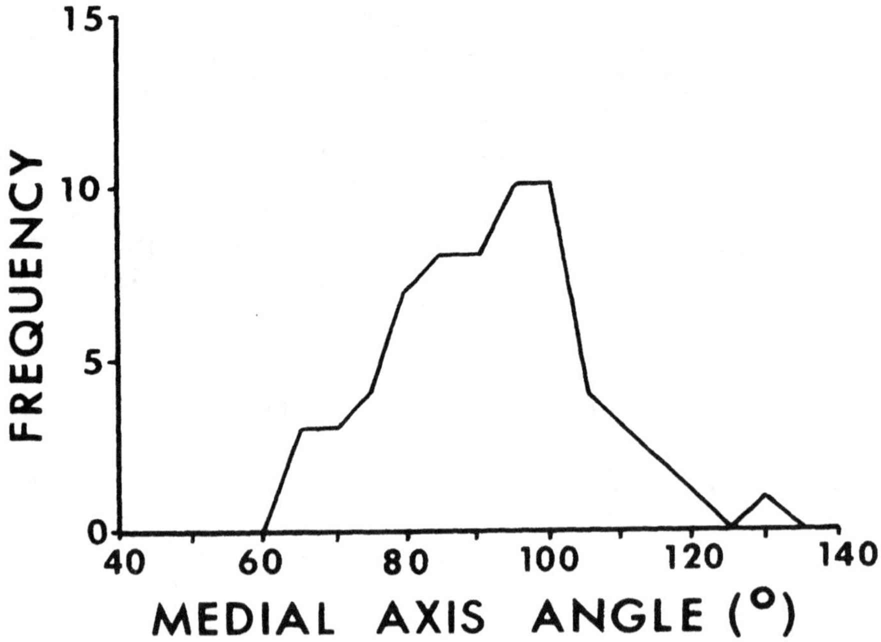

Fig. 18. Frequency distribution of medial axis angle (No. = 64).

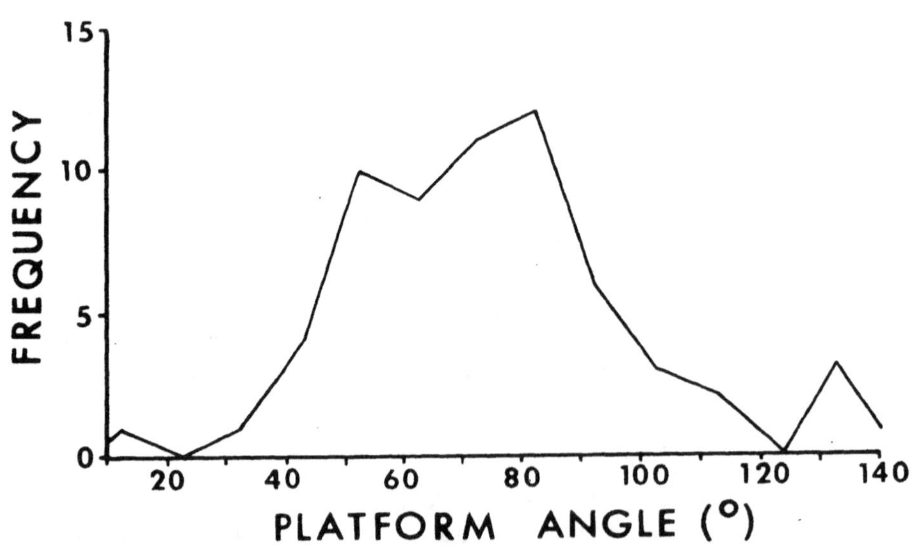

Fig. 19. Frequency distribution of platform angle (No. = 62).

6. LITHIC ARTIFACTS AND CERAMICS

The non-metric attributes recorded for the assemblage of unifacial lithic artifacts are summarized in Table 6.

Table 6. Categorical attributes of unifacial lithic artifacts

Attributes and Attribute State	No.	%
1. Maximum Width Position:	57	---
(a) Position 1	7	12.3
(b) Position 2	6	10.5
(c) Position 3	16	28.1
(d) Position 4	13	22.8
(e) Position 5	15	26.3
2. Platform Preparation:	69	---
(a) Unmodified Cortex	15	21.7
(b) Unmodified Tool Edge	15	21.7
(c) Flat	32	46.4
(d) Faceted	7	10.1
3. Platform Abrasion:	70	---
(a) Present	24	34.3
(b) Absent	46	65.7
4. Termination:	87	---
(a) Feathered	62	71.3
(b) Hinged	25	28.7
5. Dorsal Face:	135	---
(a) Unmodified Cortex	10	7.4
(b) Cortex with Flaking	9	6.7
(c) Flat	25	18.5
(d) Flaked	91	67.4
6. Condition:	125	---
(a) Complete	52	41.6
(b) Proximal Fragment	14	11.2
(c) Distal Fragment	21	16.8
(d) Medial or Lateral Fragment	38	30.4
7. Type:	137	---
(a) Unmodified Flake	118	86.1
(b) Utilized Flake	11	8.0
(c) Retouched Flake	8	5.8

Three categorical or non-metric attributes were used to divide the unifacial lithic assemblage into a number of subsets. These attributes were condition, type and material (the latter is described in Table 4 above). The metric attributes of each subset were then compared to those of other subsets, in order to determine whether the mean values of the attributes under study are the same among all subsets. The statistical test employed was Analysis of Variance (F-test; 0.01 level of significance). The test was performed using MIDAS, Statistical Research Laboratory, University of Michigan.

No significant differences were found in any metric attribute among different subsets of artifact condition. This indicates that the average dimensions of the broken pieces are essentially the same as those of the complete specimens. As a result, the values observed for the entire assemblage (Table 5) are representative of the population of complete artifacts, despite the fact that many broken items were included in the sample.

The mean values of several metric attributes (length, width, bulbar thickness, maximum thickness and platform width) vary significantly among artifacts of different type (unmodified, utilized and retouched). The results of the Analysis of Variance are summarized in Table 7. In each case, retouched flakes had larger mean values of these attributes than utilized flakes, and utilized flakes had larger mean values than unmodified flakes.

Table 7. Metric attributes that vary significantly among unmodified, utilized and unifacially retouched artifacts

Attribute	No.	F-Statistic	Attained Significance
1. Length	134	9.08	.0002
2. Width	134	9.42	.0002
3. Bulbar Thickness	75	6.18	.0033
4. Maximum Thickness	134	8.64	.0003
5. Platform Width	68	5.23	.0077

Only one metric attribute, the maximum thickness of flakes, was found to differ significantly among categories of lithic material. The ratio of length to maximum thickness also behaved in a similar manner (see Tables 8 and 9).

Table 8. Metric attributes that vary significantly among categories of lithic material

Attribute	No.	F-Statistic	Attained Significance
1. Maximum Thickness	122	3.41	.0006
2. Log10 Max. Thickness	122	3.03	.0020
3. Length/Thickness	122	6.40	.0001
4. Log10 Length/Thickness	97	2.95	.0031

Data presented in Table 9 suggest that the flakes of probable non-local lithic materials tend to be thinner than the flakes of local materials. One obvious explanation for this rather interesting phenomenon is that local and non-local lithic materials differ in some fundamental way in their mechanical properties. This seems unlikely. Since the majority of flakes are the products of resharpening, it is possible that different techniques of trimming tool edges were used for local and non-local materials. A third explanation is that the tools made from non-local materials tended to have steeper (i.e., larger) edge angles. The basis for this suggestion is as follows.

6. LITHIC ARTIFACTS AND CERAMICS

Experiments were conducted in which steel balls of constant size were dropped from a fixed height onto massive equilateral and right-angle glass prisms (Speth 1978). These experiments were designed to investigate the effects of varying platform angle and prism size on the shape and size of hard-hammer percussion flakes. The results indicate that for prisms of comparable size, an increase in the prism angle (the counterpart of the edge of a tool) from 45° to 60° was accompanied by a significant decrease in the average thickness of flakes, and by increases in the maximum possible flake length and in the average values of the length/width and length/thickness ratios.

The results of these experiments suggest that the higher length/thickness ratios, observed among resharpening flakes of non-local materials, may be the direct outcome of trimming tools with larger average edge angles. In order to check this possibility, a very small sample of resharpening flakes from the Garnsey site, that preserved measureable remnants of the original working edge of the tool, were examined. The average edge angle of the non-local specimens was about nine degrees larger than that of the local pieces. The present sample is far too small to be conclusive, but it does at least very tentatively suggest that there may be consistent functional differences between tools made on local versus non-local materials.

Table 9. Maximum thickness and length/thickness ratio among categories of lithic material

Lithic Material	No.	Max. Thickness		Length/Thickness	
		Mean	S	Mean	S
1. Grey-tan-and-blue chert	52	3.15	2.12	4.45	2.10
2. Grey chert	12	2.54	1.61	4.48	2.50
3. Chalky white-tan chert	12	3.08	1.94	4.83	2.18
4. Milky chalcedony	9	4.17	1.70	3.59	1.21
5. Igneous	6	8.25	8.42	3.42	1.99
6. Red-yellow chert	6	4.00	1.87	3.59	1.57
7. Quartzite	6	2.42	1.80	3.79	1.63
8. Yellow-tan chalcedony	5	0.90	0.22	12.00	4.40
9. Grey chalcedony	5	1.90	1.14	6.45	4.08
10. Banded chalcedony	5	2.20	1.04	6.21	2.45

Among the unifacial lithic artifacts under discussion are a small number of utilized and retouched specimens. These include 2 complete, unifacially retouched endscrapers (Fig. 20), fragments of 6 other unifacially retouched tools and 11 flakes or fragments with evidence of utilization. Both of the endscrapers are small (about 2 cm in diameter) and very steep. There is no unambiguous evidence of hafting on either specimen. One of the endscrapers, however, is broken on the side opposite the retouch and has traces of crushing on the lateral edges adjacent to the break. Both features suggest that this specimen may have been hafted and that it broke during use, either at or within the haft (F-9/S).

Fig. 20. Endscrapers (left, EF-4/S; right, F-9/S) from the Garnsey site (note that scale is in inches).

Edge Characteristics of Tools: The obvious limitations of the very small sample of unifacially and bifacially retouched tools and utilized flakes from the Garnsey site prompted a close examination of the unmodified flakes, in the hope that additional inferences might be made concerning tool use. Previous work by Frison (1968) has indicated that tool utilization patterns often may be inferred from an analysis of the resharpening flakes. As has been previously noted, the majority of the lithic artifacts from the Garnsey site are believed to represent the biproducts of trimming the edges of various tools. Eighteen of the unmodified flakes (representing a minimum of 12 tools) showed unmistakable traces on their platforms of the original working edge of the tool from which they were removed. At least 8 of these trimming flakes were removed from bifacial tools of one sort or another. In most cases, the edge angle of the original tool, patterns of use-wear and characteristics of the retouch could be ascertained. For this reason, these attributes of the 18 resharpening flakes were included in the analysis of the otherwise extremely small collection of utilized and retouched tools. The biface (0-2/16) discussed above also has been included.

The angles formed by the utilized and retouched edges of the tools varied widely, from a minimum of 20° to a maximum of 90°. The frequency distribution of these edge angles (Fig. 21) shows several modes, suggesting that the edge angles tend to cluster around certain values. There are two, and perhaps three distinct modes (20°-30°; 40°-50°; and 75°-85°). The first mode (i.e., the smallest edge angles) corresponds almost exclusively to the utilized pieces. The second mode contains both utilized and retouched pieces. And finally, the third mode (i.e., the largest edge angles) consists almost entirely of retouched tools, both unifacial and bifacial (Table 10; Fig. 22).

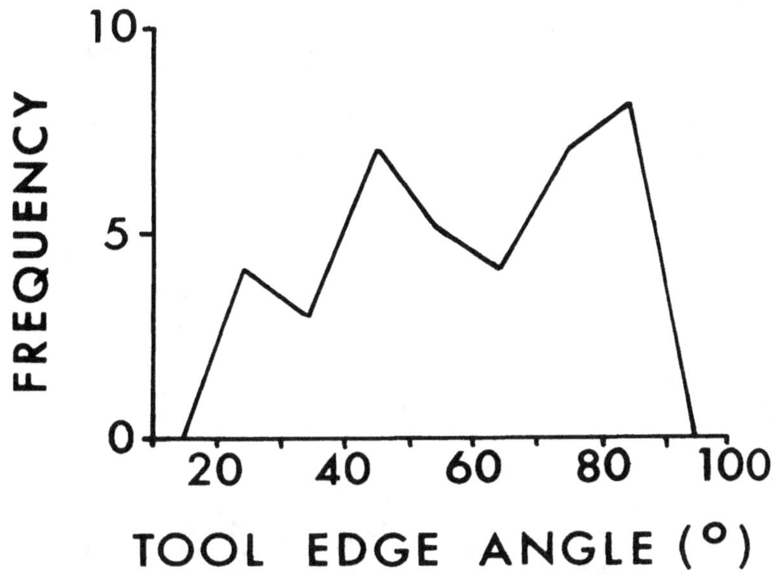

Fig. 21. Frequency distribution of edge angles of all tools (No. = 38).

Table 10. Edge angles of utilized and retouched tools

Tool Type	No. Edges	Mean	S	Min.	Max.
1. Utilized	11	37.7°	16.3°	20°	80°
2. Unifacially Retouched	12	63.3°	16.7°	35°	90°
3. Bifacially Retouched	11	65.5°	16.2°	30°	90°
4. All Tools Combined	37	56.6°	20.0°	20°	90°

Several distinct patterns of macroscopic edge damage were observed on the working edges of tools. These were classified into four types: abrasion only, irregular chipping, microretouch and scalar retouch (the latter two forms of retouch, as noted earlier, correspond approximately to types "g" and "e," respectively, as illustrated in Brézillon 1971:109). Mean edge angles differed markedly among subsets of tools that exhibited different forms of edge damage (Table 11).

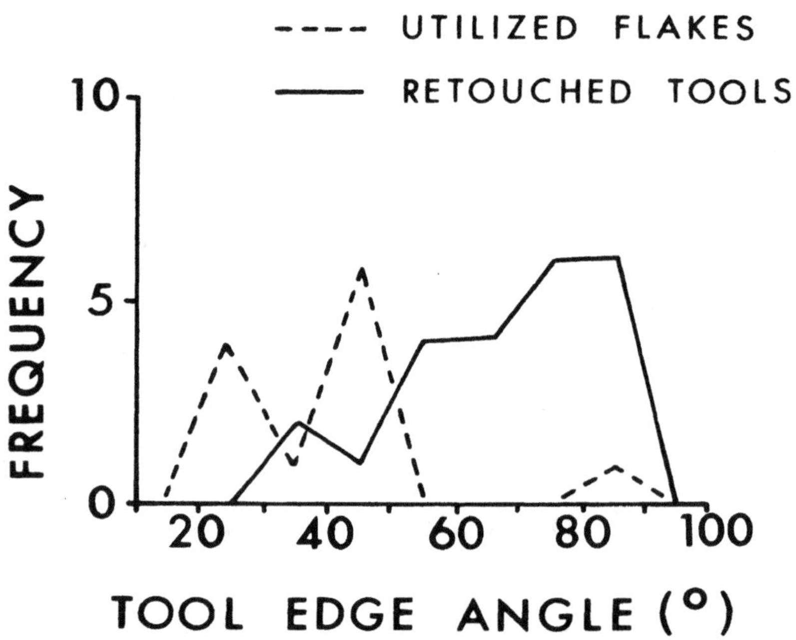

Fig. 22. Comparison of edge angles of utilized (No. = 12) and retouched (No. = 22) tools.

Table 11. Edge angles of tools grouped according to pattern of edge damage

Damage Pattern	No. Edges	Mean	S	Min.	Max.
1. Abrasion Only	6	55.0°	13.8°	40°	80°
2. Irregular Chipping	9	33.9°	10.5°	20°	50°
3. Microretouch	11	56.8°	18.1°	35°	80°
4. Scalar Retouch	11	75.9°	13.8°	60°	90°

Macroscopic abrasion was observed on the working edges of 53% (19 of 36) of the lithic tools. This percentage remained more or less constant among all tool types (i.e., utilized, unifacially retouched and bifacially retouched), regardless of edge angle or pattern of retouch or chipping. The frequency of abrasion also was similar among complete tools, fragmentary tools and unquestionable resharpening flakes. The abrasion, therefore, appears to be the result of tool use and not the product of platform preparation or post-depositional disturbance.

6. LITHIC ARTIFACTS AND CERAMICS

To generalize, it appears that the tools from the Garnsey site tend to cluster into three groups. The first group is typified by unifacially utilized flakes, with mean edge angles around 30° and with edge damage in the form of irregular chipping. The second group includes both utilized and retouched tools (unifacial and bifacial), with mean edge angles around 55° and with edge damage in the form of microretouch and/or abrasion. The third group is typified by retouched tools, with mean edge angles around 75° and with damage in the form of scalar retouch. Approximately half of the tools in each group have observable abrasion in addition to other edge damage.

These three groups of tools probably represent different functional categories. A study of Paleo-Indian tools by Wilmsen (1970) reached similar conclusions. Wilmsen observed three modal edge angles in the Paleo-Indian assemblages (26°-35°; 46°-55°; and 66°-75°). Although the Garnsey site material is almost 11,000 years younger, comparable functional categories appear to be present. Most of the Garnsey tools probably relate to a relatively limited set of activities concerned with the procurement and initial processing (butchering) of bison. Since only a small proportion of the Garnsey site has been investigated, however, other sets of activities performed at the site may remain to be documented.

7. CONCLUSIONS

In light of the evidence presently available, the Garnsey site appears to have been the locus of periodic ambushes of bison that were grazing in the wash or that were attracted to the area by the spring. Other methods of procurement, however, cannot be ruled out entirely at this stage in the analysis. Procurement activities at the site were most intense during the 15th or early 16th century, although kills may have occurred somewhat earlier and probably continued to be made, at least intermittently, into the early historic period.

The seasonal timing of procurement activities at the site cannot be specified precisely until a more detailed analysis of the dentitions has been completed.

An almost equal proportion of males and females were taken, and the majority of these were relatively old adults. At least one neonatal animal was killed. The other immature bison taken at the site were between the ages of one and two. Prime adults between the ages of three and six or seven are conspicuously underrepresented.

In general, the animals appear to have been heavily butchered. Only one front-end was left intact. The other carcasses were almost totally disarticulated. Several skeletal elements commonly were broken during the butchering process. These include the lumbar vertebrae, sacra, ribs, scapulae, radii, pelves and tibias. Other elements seldom showed direct evidence of butchering. These include the skulls, mandibles, metacarpals and metatarsals. Many post-cranial elements are underrepresented, suggesting that certain portions of the carcasses may have been preferentially removed from the kill area for further processing or for transport elsewhere. For example, bones from rear-leg units tend to be somewhat less well-represented than those from front-leg units. Since only a relatively small proportion of the site has been sampled, this difference may derive largely from sampling bias or from differential preservation.

This synthesis obviously is far from complete, and much remains to be learned about the Garnsey site. Forthcoming excavations should clarify many of the problems raised in the present study concerning methods of procurement and processing, seasonality and frequency of procurement activities, meat yields and so forth.

Continued excavation at the Garnsey site is one aspect of a broader program of archaeological research in the Bottomless Lakes area, directed toward the investigation of local subsistence and settlement systems during the late prehistoric and early historic periods.

An important focus of this work concerns the apparent transition, during the 13th and 14th centuries, from sedentary horticultural adaptations to semi- or non-sedentary hunting and gathering adaptations, based heavily on the procurement of bison (Jelinek 1967; Collins 1966, 1971). Most studies of hunter-gatherer and horticultural adaptations have focused on the unidirectional shift from simple, non-sedentary systems to more complex, sedentary ones. The ongoing research in the Bottomless Lakes area should contribute to our understanding of cultural evolution in the Southwest and elsewhere, by examining the conditions that favor adaptive shifts in the opposite direction, that is, toward less complex and less sedentary hunting and gathering adaptations.

APPENDIX I. BISON REMAINS FROM THE GARNSEY SITE

APPENDIX I

KEY TO FAUNAL TABLES

I. General Comments on Tables

A. All specimens listed in these tables are bison, unless specifically noted otherwise.
B. All measurements are given in centimeters.
C. Most of the abbreviations used as column headings in each table are explained in footnotes at the end of the table; a few headings that are used in all or most of the tables are explained below.
D. The symbols used as entries in the tables are explained below. Often these symbols are accompanied by a footnote explaining some aspect of the particular entry; such footnotes are found at the end of each table.

II. Specific Table Headings and Entries

A. Prov. (Provenience)
1. F-3/2 (Unit F-3; Item 2)
2. Bkdt (Recovered in backdirt; no exact provenience)
3. F-3/S (Unit F-3; recovered in screen; provenience approximate)
4. F-3/Blk (Unit F-3; removed from bulk)
5. F-3/2A (Unit F-3; Item 2A; two or more items with same number)

B. Side (of body)
1. F (Front)
2. Re (Rear)
3. L (Left)
4. R (Right)
5. "L" (Left side of foot; side of animal unknown)
6. "R" (Right side of foot; side of animal unknown)
7. I (Internal side of foot; side of animal known)
8. E (External side of foot, side of animal known)
9. C (Center or midline of foot; side of animal unknown)
10. P (Periphery or edge of foot; side of animal unknown)

C. Port. (Portion)
1. Ab (Abaxial)
2. An (Anterior)
3. Ax (Axial)
4. B (Vertebral body only)
5. Bl (Blade fragment only)
6. Bo (Border fragment; side unknown)
7. C (Complete)
8. CB (Scapula missing most of blade)
9. Cd (Caudal)
10. Cr (Cranial)
11. D (Distal)
12. Da (Damaged)

C. Port. (cont.)

13. De (Distal epiphysis)
14. Di (Diaphysis)
15. Do (Dorsal)
16. L (Left)
17. La (Lateral)
18. LTP (Left transverse process)
19. M (Medial)
20. Ms (Midsection of specimen)
21. P (Proximal)
22. Pcd (Caudal vertebral pad)
23. Pcr (Cranial vertebral pad)
24. Pe (Proximal epiphysis)
25. Po (Posterior)
26. R (Right)
27. Rs (Restored)
28. RTP (Right transverse process)
29. SP (Complete spinous process)
30. SPdo (Spinous process dorsal section)
31. SPms (Spinous process midsection)
32. Spn (Spine)
33. SPs (Unfused spinous process summit)
34. SPv (Spinous process ventral section)
35. TP (Transverse process; side unknown)
36. V (Ventral)
37. Vo (Volar or plantar)

D. But. (Butchering)

1. 0 (None evident)
2. 1 (Breakage and/or cut-marks evident; usually described in footnote at base of table)

E. Fus. (Fusion)

1. Fus.(P) (Fusion of proximal end)
2. Fus.(D) (Fusion of distal end)
3. Fus.(Cr) (Fusion of cranial pad)
4. Fus.(Cd) (Fusion of caudal pad)
5. Fus.(Msc) (Fusion of medial sacral crest)
6. Fus.(Lsc) (Fusion of lateral sacral crest)
7. Fus.(Sgt) (Fusion of supraglenoid tubercle)
8. 0 (Unfused)
9. 0.5 (Fusing)
10. 1 (Fused)

F. Other Symbols

1. --- (Indeterminate or not relevant)
2. (1.35) (Measurement is close approximation of real value)
3. [1.35] (Measurement applies to broken, damaged or incomplete specimen; measurement does not reflect real value for complete specimen)

Table 12a. [a]Skull (Part I)

Prov.	Port.	But.	b_1	b_2	b_3	b_4	b_5	b_6	b_7	b_8	b_9
"BLM"	[c]Da	0	[34.9]	[34.9]	---	---	---	[d][7.0]	[d][27.0]	24.1	13.0
CC-0035/1	[e]R,An	0	---	---	---	---	---	---	---	---	---
E-19/5	[f]Da	0	[g](50.0)	[g](50.0)	[g](14.0)	[g](15.5)	[g](13.5)	5.3	17.3	20.4	11.3
EF-9, 10/S	[h]An	(1)	---	---	---	---	---	---	---	---	---
F-0024/1	[i]L,Po	0	---	---	(20.5)	(25.0)	(17.5)	(7.3)	(24.3)	---	---
F-8/2	[j]Po	(1)	---	---	---	---	---	---	---	---	---
F-9/28	[k]Da	0	[36.7]	[36.7]	---	---	---	5.6	17.0	20.6	11.5
G-11, 12/S	[l]Po	1	---	---	---	---	---	---	---	---	---
G-13/5	[m]C	0	[51.8]	[51.8]	13.0	14.3	12.3	6.9	22.1	24.5	13.8
H-2/1	[n]Da	0	---	---	[o](11.0)	[o](13.0)	[o](10.5)	5.0	16.3	20.6	11.7
H-16/10	[p]Po	(1)	[40.8]	[40.8]	---	---	---	[q](7.8)	[q](24.4)	[q](22.6)	12.5
H-16/10 (Assoc.)	[r]Po	1	---	---	---	---	---	---	---	---	---
H-18/5	[s]Po	(0)	---	---	---	---	---	---	---	---	10.8
H-27/1	[t]R,An	0	---	---	---	---	---	---	---	---	---
I-5/1	[u]L,Po	0	---	---	[10.2]	[12.5]	[10.0]	5.0	16.2	---	---
O-3/16	[v]L,Po	0	---	---	[13.8]	[16.0]	[13.5]	[6.9]	[25.0]	---	14.3
O-4/4	[w]Da	0	---	---	[x](11.2)	[x](11.5)	[x](11.0)	5.1	16.3	(17.9)	---
P-3/5 (P4/7)	[y]Da	0	[z](44.0)	[z](44.5)	---	---	[z](12.0)	5.5	17.1	19.5	10.9
P-3/45	[aa]R,An	(0)	---	---	---	---	---	---	---	---	---
P-3/69	[bb]Po	1	---	---	---	---	---	---	---	---	13.7
P-3, 4/S	[cc]Po	1	---	---	---	---	---	---	---	---	---
P-4/28	[dd]R,Po	(1)	---	---	(17.9)	---	(15.7)	[ee][4.7]	[ee][22.5]	---	---

[a]See Parts II, III and IV of Table for additional measurements and observations on skulls.

[b]1 (Spread of Horn Cores, Tip to Tip); 2 (Greatest Spread of Cores on Outside Curve); 3 (Core Length on Upper Curve, Tip to Burr); 4 (Core Length on Lower Curve, Tip to Burr); 5 (Length, Tip of Core to Upper Base at Burr); 6 (Vertical Diameter of Horn Core); 7 (Circumference of Horn Core); 8 (Greatest Width of Auditory Openings); 9 (Width of Condyles) (after Skinner and Kaisen 1947).

[c]Skull prior to removal nearly complete; posterior region partially exposed in arroyo wall; specimen removed by graduate student ca. 1974-75 (?) at request of local Bureau of Land Management archaeologist for identification; horn cores from approximately burr to tip destroyed in process of removal.

[d]Values for vertical diameter and circumference of horn core are approximations and are probably somewhat too high; measurements were taken between burr and base, but not perpendicular to longitudinal axis of horn core.

Table 12a. (cont.)

[e]Right maxilla fragment from first molar forward, including adjacent palate and right premaxilla; specimen removed from arroyo wall.

[f]Nearly complete skull; tips of both horn cores damaged; entire skull compressed dorso-ventrally.

[g]Tip of both horn cores damaged; values given in Table for Measurements 1-5 are estimates; actual values were (1) 46.6, (2) 46.6, (3) 13.4, (4) 12.6, (5) 13.0.

[h]Small anterior fragment of left nasal bone only.

[i]Skull fragment exposed in arroyo wall; specimen consists of left posterior section only (left horn core, frontal, orbit, occipital condyle and jugular process).

[j]Rear and right (subhorn) portions of parietal only.

[k]Complete skull; horn-core tips damaged during excavation; specimen collapsed during transport; articulated with mandibles F-9/56AB.

[l]Unfused, right jugular process only, broken from remainder of occipital bone.

[m]Nearly complete skull; right horn core and left premaxilla broken off, perhaps during butchering.

[n]Skull exposed in arroyo wall; specimen complete prior to exposure; when discovered, right longitudinal half of skull had collapsed into arroyo; right horn core completely destroyed.

[o]Tip of left horn core slightly damaged; values given in Table for Measurements 3-5 are estimates; actual values were (3) 10.2, (4) 12.6, (5) 10.0.

[p]Posterior portion of skull; specimen consists of complete occipital bone, rear and left (subhorn) parietal, all of left and part of right frontal, basal stub of left horn core, slab-like ventral stub of right horn core, and small portion of dorsal rim of left orbit.

[q]Values given in Table for Measurements 6-8 are probably slightly smaller than true values due to exfoliation of horn-core surface.

[r]Right occipital condyle only; found against right (subhorn) parietal of Skull H-16/10.

[s]Complete, unfused occipital bone only.

[t]Right maxilla fragment from third molar to fourth premolar, including portion of adjacent palate; removed from arroyo wall.

[u]Skull fragment removed from arroyo wall; specimen consists of left posterior section only (rear parietal, portion of occipital bone excluding condyles and jugular processes, basal portion of left horn core, complete left frontal and left orbit).

[v]Skull fragment exposed in arroyo wall; specimen consists of left posterior section only (basal portion of left horn core, complete occipital bone, rear and left parietal, complete left orbit, left and portion of right frontal).

[w]Skull partially exposed in arroyo wall; specimen complete except for right horn core; specimen deformed, particularly in maxillary region.

[x]Values for Measurements 3-5 in Table are estimates; actual values were (3) 10.7, (4) 11.0, (5) 10.5.

Table 12a. (cont.)

[y]Skull nearly complete; badly corroded; horns and premaxillae damaged during excavation and transport; palate and teeth smashed, probably during butchering.

[z]Values estimated from photographs with included scale.

[aa]Right maxilla fragment from third molar forward, including adjacent palate and right premaxilla.

[bb]Nearly complete, fused occipital bone; both jugular processes broken off.

[cc]Right, fused jugular process only.

[dd]Skull consists of right posterior section only (complete right horn core, portion of right frontal, and small portion of dorsal rim of right orbit).

[ee]Ventral portion of horn core badly exfoliated (part of ventral portion may have been cleaved off during butchering process); damage to core rendered measurement of vertical core diameter and core circumference impossible; transverse diameter of horn core not affected by damage.

Table 12b. [a]Skull (Part II)

Prov.	[b]10	[b]11	[b]12	[b]13	[b]14	[b]15	[b]16	[b]17	[b]18	[b]19	[b]20
"BLM"	---	---	[c][8.3]	[d](25.5)	28.8	32.8	23.4	17.7	11.5	[e](15.1)	[e]9.7
CC-0035/1	---	---	---	---	---	---	---	---	---	---	---
E-19/5	7.5	10.9	5.4	16.9	22.2	27.3	19.6	16.9	10.0	14.5	8.7
EF-9, 10/S	---	---	---	---	---	---	---	---	---	---	---
F-0024/1	---	---	(8.0)	---	---	---	---	---	---	---	---
F-8/2	---	---	---	---	---	---	---	---	---	---	---
F-9/28	7.6	10.8	5.2	(17.0)	20.6	26.3	---	---	---	14.8	9.2
G-11, 12/S	---	---	---	---	---	---	---	---	---	---	---
G-13/5	9.6	13.0	8.0	23.0	27.1	33.1	23.8	[f]17.7	10.8	(13.8)	(8.0)
H-2/1	---	---	5.5	---	---	---	---	[f](16.4)	---	14.0	8.6
H-16/10	---	---	(8.2)	---	---	---	---	---	---	---	---
H-16/10 (Assoc.)	---	---	---	---	---	---	---	---	---	---	---
H-18/5	---	---	---	---	---	---	---	---	---	---	---
H-27/1	---	---	---	---	---	---	---	---	---	---	[g](9.1)
I-5/1	(6.9)	---	5.2	---	---	---	---	---	---	---	---
O-3/16	(7.4)	(11.6)	(9.1)	---	---	---	---	---	---	---	---
O-4/4	6.1	---	5.2	---	---	[24.3]	(18.3)	(15.1)	(10.4)	14.3	9.1
P-3/5 (P-4/7)	6.1	10.2	5.5	(17.6)	21.8	(27.0)	(19.8)	17.0	---	[g](14.8)	(9.2)
P-3/45	---	---	---	---	---	---	---	---	---	[g](15.9)	---
P-3/69	---	---	---	---	---	---	---	---	---	---	---
P-3, 4/S	---	---	---	---	---	---	---	---	---	---	---
P-4/28	---	---	(8.7)	---	---	---	---	---	---	---	---

[a]See Parts I, III and IV of Table for additional measurements and observations on skulls.

[b]10 (Depth, Occipital Crest to Top of Foramen Magnum); 11 (Depth, Occipital Crest to Bottom of Foramen Magnum); 12 (Transverse Diameter of Horn Core); 13 (Width between Bases of Horn Cores); 14 (Width of Cranium between Horn Cores and Orbits); 15 (Greatest Post-Orbital Width); 16 (Anterior Orbital Width at Notch); 17 (Width of Skull at Masseteric Processes above M1); 18 (Rostral Width at Maxillary-Premaxillary Suture); 19 (P2-M3, Alveolar Length); 20 (M1-M3, Alveolar Length) (after Skinner and Kaisen 1947).

[c]Value approximate; measured between burr and base of horn core.

[d]In all cases, the values of Measurement 13 are approximate because of the difficulty of locating the base of the horn core in a consistent and replicable manner.

Table 12b. (cont.)

[e]In all cases, Measurements 19 and 20 were on the buccal side of the tooth row.

[f]Measurement approximate; obtained by standing maxillae next to each other with appropriate parts of palate in articulation.

[g]Measured from posterior alveolus (damaged) of unerupted M3.

Table 12c. [a]Skull (Part III)

Prov.	[b]O-P	[b]F-P	[b]O-T	[b]O-N	[b]M-P	[b]N-T	[b]21	[b]22
"BLM"	[c](55.0)	49.7	[c](44.6)	[c](23.9)	12.3	20.7	---	---
CC-0035/1	---	---	---	---	---	---	---	---
E-19/5	48.2	45.1	40.4	21.5	11.0	18.9	70°	[d](12°)
EF-9, 10/S	---	---	---	---	---	---	---	---
F-0024/1	---	---	---	---	---	---	---	---
F-8/2	---	---	---	---	---	---	---	---
F-9/28	(48.3)	---	39.5	21.0	---	18.5	69°	(9°)
G-11, 12/S	---	---	---	---	---	---	---	---
G-13/5	52.5	47.5	43.7	24.8	(9.4)	18.9	71°	(16°)
H-2/1	[e](48.8)	---	[e](39.4)	[e](21.0)	---	18.4	(70°)	(17°)
H-16/10	---	---	---	---	---	---	(70°)	(12°)
H-16/10 (Assoc.)	---	---	---	---	---	---	---	---
H-18/5	---	---	---	---	---	---	---	---
H-27/1	---	---	---	---	---	---	---	---
I-5/1	---	---	---	(23.0)	---	---	(71°)	(12°)
0-3/16	---	---	---	---	---	---	(73°)	(15°)
0-4/4	(48.5)	(43.6)	[39.2]	---	(11.6)	(19.0)	(69°)	(15°)
P-3/5 (P-4/7)	---	---	(39.8)	(20.5)	---	19.3	69°	(15°)
P-3/45	---	---	---	---	(8.9)	---	---	---
P-3/69	---	---	---	---	---	---	---	---
P-3, 4/S	---	---	---	---	---	---	---	---
P-4/28	---	---	---	---	---	---	---	---

[a]See Parts I, II and IV of Table for additional measurements and observations on skulls.

[b]O-P (Length, Occipital Crest to Tip of Premaxilla); F-P (Basilar Length, Foramen Magnum to Tip of Premaxilla); O-T (Length, Occipital Crest to Tip of Nasals); O-N (Length, Occipital Crest to Nasal-Frontal Suture); M-P (Length, Beyond P2 to Tip of Maxilla); N-T (Length of Nasal Bone); 21 (Angle of Posterior Divergence of Horn Core); 22 (Angle of Proximal Depression of Horn Core) (after Skinner and Kaisen 1947).

[c]Occipital crest damaged; values given in Table for Measurements O-P, O-T and O-N are estimates; actual values were (O-P) 54.1, (O-T) 43.7, (O-N) 23.0.

[d]In all cases Measurement 22 was very difficult to make in a consistent and replicable manner.

[e]Occipital crest damaged; values given in Table for Measurements O-P, O-T and O-N are estimates.

Table 12d. [a]Skull (Part IV)

Prov.	[b]Index 1	[b]Index 2	[b]Index 3	[b]Index 4	[b]Index 5	[c]Index 6	[d]Approx. Age (yrs.)	[e]Sex
"BLM"	---	---	---	---	(30.5)	87.8	[f] ≥8	M
CC-0035/1	---	---	---	---	---	---	[g]ca. 1-2	---
E-19/5	(114.8)	98.2	(80.9)	(63.1)	32.2	81.3	[h]ca. 8-10	F
EF-9, 10/S	---	---	---	---	---	---	---	---
F-0024/1	(142.9)	(91.3)	(84.4)	---	---	---	[i]Mature	M
F-8/2	---	---	---	---	---	---	[j](Mature)	---
F-9/28	---	107.7	---	---	---	78.3	[k]ca. 6-8	F
G-11, 12/S	---	---	---	---	---	---	[l]Immature	---
G-13/5	116.3	86.3	58.8	48.0	(29.1)	81.9	[m] ≥9	M
H-2/1	(123.8)	90.9	(67.5)	---	---	---	[n]ca. 8-10	F
H-16/10	---	(95.1)	---	---	---	---	[o](≥8)	M
H-16/10 (Assoc.)	---	---	---	---	---	---	---	---
H-18/5	---	---	---	---	---	---	[p]Immature	---
H-27/1	---	---	---	---	---	---	[q]ca. 1-2	---
I-5/1	---	96.2	---	---	---	---	[r]Mature	F
O-3/16	---	---	---	---	---	---	[s](≥8)	M
O-4/4	(104.6)	98.1	(68.7)	---	(32.8)	---	[t]ca. 7-8	F
P-3/5 (P-4/7)	---	100.0	---	---	---	(80.7)	[u]ca. 7-9	F
P-3/45	---	---	---	---	---	---	[v]ca. 1-2	---
P-3/69	---	---	---	---	---	---	[w](Mature)	---
P-3, 4/S	---	---	---	---	---	---	---	---
P-4/28	---	---	---	---	---	---	[x](Mature)	M

[a]See Parts I, II and III of Table for additional measurements and observations on skulls.

[b]Index 1 (Horn-Core Curvature); Index 2 (Horn-Core Compression); Index 3 (Horn-Core Proportion); Index 4 (Horn-Core Length); Index 5 (Tooth-Row Proportion) (after Skinner and Kaisen 1947).

[c]Index 6 (Index of Orbital Protrusion (after Guthrie 1966, cited in Wilson 1974).

[d]Age estimates of upper dentitions based on eruption and wear sequences published by Wilson (1974) and by Frison et al. (1978); where dentitions are absent, assignment of male skulls to broad, relative age classes based on degree of fusion of parietofrontal and frontal sutures, rugosity of orbits, prominence of burr at base of horn cores and so forth, as described by Skinner and Kaisen (1947) and Shackleton et al. (1975).

Table 12d. (cont.)

[e]Sex of skulls based on clear bimodality of horn-core transverse diameters; comparable bimodality is evident in other measures.

[f]All permanent teeth fully erupted and in full wear; (left) P2, M1 missing (post-mortem), lingual side of P4 damaged; (right) P2, P3, P4, M1 missing (post-mortem); parietofrontal suture completely closed and no longer visible; frontal suture closed but entirely visible; orbital rim highly rugose.

[g]DP2 shed or lost, P2 erupting; DP3 and DP4 in place; maxilla older than H-27/1 (DP4 style slightly more worn); maxilla also older than P-3/45 (DP3 more cupped and lingual enamel line higher).

[h]All permanent teeth fully erupted and in full wear; all teeth present; parietofrontal suture completely closed and no longer visible; frontal suture closed but entirely visible, orbital rim only slightly rugose.

[i]Dentition entirely missing; orbital rim highly rugose; burr on horn core pronounced.

[j]Size and thickness of parietal fragment suggest mature individual; age assignment tenuous.

[k]All permanent teeth fully erupted and in full wear; all teeth present; parietofrontal and frontal sutures entirely visible; orbital rim smooth.

[l]Unfused.

[m]All permanent teeth fully erupted and in full wear; (left) P2, P3, P4 missing (post-mortem); (right) P2, P3, P4, M1 missing (post-mortem?); some possible bone resorption on right side; parietofrontal suture completely closed and no longer visible; frontal suture no longer visible posteriorly; orbital rim highly rugose.

[n]All permanent teeth fully erupted and in full wear; all teeth present; parietofrontal and frontal sutures visible; orbital rim smooth.

[o]Dentition entirely missing, frontal suture no longer visible posteriorly.

[p]Unfused.

[q]DP4 in place, M2 almost completely erupted; M3 unerupted; maxilla younger than CC-0035/1 (DP4 style slightly less worn); maxilla older than P-3/45 (M2 slightly further erupted and more worn).

[r]Dentition entirely missing, parietofrontal suture not entirely visible; orbital rim smooth.

[s]Dentition entirely missing; parietofrontal and frontal sutures completely closed and no longer visible.

[t]All permanent teeth fully erupted and in full wear; (left) P2, P3, P4, M1 missing (post-mortem); (right) P2, P3, P4 missing (post-mortem); parietofrontal and frontal sutures entirely visible; orbital rim smooth.

[u]All permanent teeth fully erupted and in full wear; (left) P2 missing (post-mortem), P3 and P4 smashed to level of alveoli, M1 and M2 partially smashed; (right) P2, P3, P4, and M1 missing (post-mortem), M2 smashed to level of alveolus, M3 partially smashed; damage to teeth and palate probably due to butchering; parietofrontal suture closed and barely visible; frontal suture fully visible; orbital rim smooth.

Table 12d. (cont.)

[v]DP2 missing (shed or lost); P2 unerupted; DP3 and DP4 in place; M1 fully erupted; M2 erupting; M3 unerupted; maxilla younger than CC-0035/1 (DP3 less cupped and lingual enamel line lower); maxilla younger than H-27/1 (M2 less erupted and less worn).

[w]Fused.

[x]Dentition entirely missing; burr on horn core pronounced.

Table 13a. [a]Mandible (Part I)

Prov.	Side	Port.	But.	b_1	b_2	b_3	b_4	b_5	b_6	b_7	b_8	b_9
E-10/4	L	[c]C	0	39.72	43.26	11.54	27.70	27.15	33.08	15.78	10.07	5.53
E-22/1	L	[d]Da	0	[15.35]	[16.20]	(6.25)	---	12.35	14.77	---	---	(6.13)
F-4/2	R	[e]C	0	38.40	(39.95)	12.72	(25.40)	27.30	33.35	(14.67)	(9.22)	(6.34)
F-9/56A	L	[f]C	0	39.40	40.48	12.05	26.75	27.60	33.95	15.68	10.15	5.59
F-9/56B	R	[g]C	0	39.53	40.75	12.11	26.73	27.75	33.78	15.72	10.22	5.51
H-2/1	L	[h]Po	(1)	---	---	---	---	---	---	---	---	---
H-18/3	R	[i]C	0	37.25	38.83	11.42	25.90	25.80	31.72	14.67	9.61	4.88
0-4/5	L	[j]Da	0	---	---	(12.80)	---	(27.80)	---	(14.90)	(8.10)	(5.85)
0-4/17	R	[k]C	1	(34.10)	(36.15)	[9.69]	(24.00)	[24.70]	[31.00]	(16.05)	(9.09)	(6.17)

[a]See Part II of this Table for additional measurements and observations on mandibles.

[b]1 (Length from Angle to Infradentale); 2 (Length from Condyle to Infradentale); 3 (Length from Angle to M3); 4 (Length of Horizontal Ramus between M3 and Infradentale); 5 (Length from Angle to front of P2); 6 (Length from Angle to Mental Foramen); 7 (Length of Cheektooth Row); 8 (Length of Molar Row); 9 (Length of Premolar Row) (after von den Driesch 1976).

[c]All incisors and canine missing (post-mortem).

[d]Damaged during excavation; partially restored; lingual side missing; oral portion with incisors and canine destroyed.

[e]All incisors and canine missing (post-mortem).

[f]I1 missing (post-mortem).

[g]Canine missing (post-mortem).

[h]Fragment of ascending ramus only; exposed in arroyo; condylar process complete; coronoid process and anterior border of ramus broken off; ramus broken from rest of mandible along relatively straight surface just below mandibular foramen.

[i]All incisors, canine and P3 missing (post-mortem); P2 and M3 damaged (post-mortem).

[j]Severe weathering damage due to exposure in arroyo; ventral border, all incisors and canine, their sockets and symphysis lost (post-mortem); P2, aboral half of M2, and M3 missing (post-mortem).

[k]Coronoid process butchered off; incisors and canine, their sockets, and most of symphysis missing (probably intentionally broken off); all premolars and molars present; all teeth except M3 smashed off at level of alveoli; mandible appears to have been used as chopping or hammering tool.

Table 13b. [a]Mandible (Part II)

Prov.	[b]10	[b]10A	[b]11	[b]12	[b]13	[b]14	[b]15A	[b]15B	[b]15C	[c]Approx. Age(yrs.)	[n]W	[o]Sex
E-10/4	4.36	1.55	12.47	14.60	14.80	20.75	7.39	[l]5.51	[l]4.48	[d]ca. 5.5-6.5	7.45	M
E-22/1	---	---	[3.05]	4.98	5.39	[7.23]	(4.90)	[m](3.62)	[m](2.09)	[e]neonatal	---	---
F-4/2	3.96	1.79	(11.12)	14.85	14.15	19.40	7.17	[m]3.76	[l]3.88	[f]≥10	6.64	F
F-9/56A	4.23	1.58	11.15	14.70	(14.80)	(20.25)	7.40	[l]5.11	[l]4.40	[g]ca. 6-7	6.92	F
F-9/56B	4.22	1.57	11.42	14.60	14.35	19.50	7.44	[l]5.09	[l]4.46	[h]ca. 6-7	6.94	F
H-2/1	---	---	---	---	---	---	---	---	---	---	---	---
H-18/3	(4.28)	1.62	(9.01)	15.53	14.66	19.60	7.25	[l]5.26	[l]4.53	[i]ca. 7-8	6.95	F
0-4/5	---	---	---	[14.45]	[13.25]	[19.00]	[6.30]	[l]---	[l]---	[j]≥10	(7.35)	(M)
0-4/17	(4.10)	(1.90)	(8.40)	13.95	---	---	8.03	[l]5.42	[l]3.99	[k]ca. 3-4	7.81	M

[a]See Part I of Table for additional measurements and observations on mandibles.

[b]10 (Length of M3); 10A (Breadth of M3); 11 (Length of Diastema P2-I4); 12 (Aboral Height of Ramus); 13 (Middle Height of Ramus); 14 (Oral Height of Ramus); 15A (Height of Mandible behind M3); 15B (Height of Mandible in front of M1); 15C (Height of Mandible in front of P2) (after von den Driesch 1976).

[c]Ages presented in table are tentative and subject to revision as sample is increased by subsequent excavation; ages based on eruption sequence and wear (see Frison et al. 1976).

[d]All permanent teeth fully erupted and in full wear.

[e]DP2 partially erupted; DP3 and DP4 fully erupted; very light wear on DP4; M1 visible but not erupted.

[f]All permanent teeth fully erupted and in full wear; P2, P3 and P4 missing (ante-mortem); loss of premolars accompanied by bone resorption; M1 lost (probably post-mortem); M2 worn flat and smooth below enamel, leaving no trace of cusps or fossettes; M3 worn almost to base of enamel, nearly obliterating prefossette.

[g]All permanent teeth fully erupted and in full wear; articulated with skull F-9/28.

[h]All permanent teeth fully erupted and in full wear; articulated with skull F-9/28.

[i]All permanent teeth fully erupted and in full wear.

[j]M1, oral half of M2 and P4 lost (ante-mortem); considerable bone resorption; ramus swept back more than in other mandibles, perhaps result of bone resorption.

[k]All permanent premolars and molars fully erupted; wear on facets I-IV and light wear on facets V and VI of M3 (see Frison et al. 1976).

[l]Measured on lingual side.

[m]Measured on buccal side.

[n]W (Width of mandible below M3) (after Reher 1974).

[o]Based on values of W (see Reher 1974); results should be used with caution due to small sample size.

Table 14. Hyoid

Prov.	Side	Port.	But.	[a]GLS	[a]GLT	[a]GLSA
A-2/1	R	Da	0	[11.47]	[2.46]	(3.75)
E-3/9	R	[b]Ms	1	[12.35]	[4.08]	[3.53]
EF-5, 6/S	---	[c]Ms	1	[3.25]	---	---
F-9/28A	R	C	0	15.00	4.83	3.51
F-9/28B	L	C	0	15.02	5.05	3.55
F-10/3	R	Da	0	[11.86]	5.15	[3.21]
G-11/7	L	[d]Da	(0)	[6.58]	[3.33]	---
H-14/10	L	Da	0	[8.42]	[4.18]	[2.03]

[a]GLS (Greatest Length of Stylohyoid); GLT (Greatest Length of Tympanohyoid); GLSA (Greatest Length of Stylohyoid Angle).

[b]Anterior end and tympanohyoid arm missing; stylohyoid angle damaged.

[c]Fragment of stylohyoid near base of stylohyoid angle and tympanohyoid arm.

[d]Anterior end of stylohyoid missing; hyoid of an immature individual.

Table 15. Miscellaneous loose teeth (incisor/canine)

Prov.	[a]Comment
E-1/8	D
E-10/13	P
EF-3, 4/S (5/30/77)	P; heavily worn
EF-8/S (6/5/77)	D
EF-9, 10/S (6/15/77)	P; heavily worn
EF-9, 10/S (6/16/77)	P
EF-11/S (6/28/77)	(P)
EF-11/S (7/1/77)	P
EF-25, 26/S (7/18/77)	P
F-5/4	P
F-7/2	P
F-9/(Assoc. with F-9/56)	P
F-10/27	D
F-10/30	P
GH-11, 12/S (7/15/77)	P; heavily worn
GH-19, 20/S (8/3/77)	P
#715 Alidade Foresite	P

[a]D (Deciduous); P (Permanent).

Table 16. Miscellaneous loose teeth (molar/premolar)

Prov.	[a]Comment
Bkdt (1977)	---
Bkdt (1977)	P2
E-2/5	P
E-9/2	P
E-10/11	P
E-12/1	P
EF/Bkdt (1977)	M1; upper
EF-4/S (5/31/77)	P2
EF-9, 10/S (6/13/77)	---
EF-11/S (6/28/77)	P; unerupted
EF-11, 14/S (6/15/77)	Heavily worn
F-9/34	P
F-10/S (6/14/77)	P2
G-5, 6/S (6/4/77)	---
G-12/3	---
G-14/3	P
G-21/4	M; upper
GH-16, 18/S (7/18/77)	---
H-18/10	P; unerupted
OP-2, 4/S (8/4/77)	P2

[a]M (Molar); P (Premolar).

Table 17. [a]Miscellaneous tooth fragments

Prov.	No.	Comments
D-11, 12/S (7/11/77)	3	
D-12/S (7/12/77)	1	
E-3, 4/S (6/4/77)	1	
E-5, 6/S (6/7/77)	4	
E-8/5	2	
E-9/S (6/14/77)	1	
E-11/S (6/27/77)	3	
EF-1, 2/S (5/30/77)	2	
EF-1, 2/S (5/31/77)	1	
EF-4/S (5/31/77)	3	
EF-4, 5/S (5/31/77)	1	
EF-5, 6/S (6/6/77)	2	
EF-7, 8/S (6/6/77)	1	
EF-9, 10/S (6/13/77)	5	
EF-9, 10/S (6/14/77)	7	
EF-9, 10/S (6/16/77)	3	
EF-11/S (6/28/77)	4	
EF-11/S (7/11/77)	1	
EF-11, 12/S (6/26/77)	2	
EF-11, 14/S (6/15/77)	2	
EF-22/S (7/25/77)	1	
EF-25, 26/S (7/18/77)	1	
F-1, 2/S (Lower Gravel)	1	
F-3/S (6/3/77)	4	
F-5/4	2	

Table 17. (cont.)

Prov.	No.	Comments
G-5, 6/S (6/4/77)	2	
G-13/S (7/11/77)	1	
G-21, 22/S (8/3/77)	1	
GH-11, 12/S (7/15/77)	2	
GH-11, 12/S (7/16/77)	4	
GH-11, 12/S (7/17/77)	1	
GH-13, 14/S (7/11/77)	2	
GH-13, 14/S (7/12/77)	6	
GH-13, 14/S (7/16/77)	3	
GH-16/S (7/19/77)	1	
GH-16, 18/S (7/8/77)	1	
GH-16, 18/S (7/18/77)	1	
GH-16, 19/S (7/5/77)	1	
GH-17/S (7/9/77)	1	
GH-18/S (7/17/77)	1	
H-2/1	1	
H-16/S. Wall/S (7/11/77)	1	
H-18/14	1	With small maxilla fragment
H-27/1	1	
OP-2, 4/S (8/1/77)	1	
OP-2, 4/S (8/4/77)	1	
OP-2, 4/S (8/5/77)	2	
OP-2, 4/S (8/9/77)	3	
P-3, 4/S½/S (6/11/77)	3	
P-4/7	1	

[a]Unidentifiable fragments only.

Table 18. Atlas

Prov.	Port.	But.	Fus.	[a]GB	[a]GL	[a]BFcr	[a]BFcd	[a]GLF	[a]H
F-0024/5	L	[b]1	1	[10.00]	[12.00]	---	---	---	[10.00]
F-9/55	C	0	1	15.35	10.70	11.10	9.94	8.97	9.48
G-13/1	C	0	1	(17.13)	(11.62)	12.60	10.99	9.93	(10.39)
H-2/1	R	[c]1	1	(14.70)	(10.01)	11.58	[9.15]	9.62	9.18
O-2/4	L	[d]0	1	[18.88]	(13.20)	[12.81]	[10.96]	10.58	[10.81]
O-3/25	C	0	1	19.70	13.51	12.59	11.85	10.59	(9.68)
O-3/27	C	0	1	14.55	10.90	10.70	9.62	9.55	[8.10]
P-2/2	C	0	[e](1)	15.52	10.85	12.31	10.39	9.62	9.51
P-2/22	R	[f]1	---	---	---	---	---	---	---
Q-3/5	C	0	1	20.99	13.85	13.05	11.42	11.05	11.10
Q-4/1	R	[g](1)	---	---	---	---	---	---	---
R-002/1	C	0	[e](1)	(11.70)	8.00	(9.65)	8.21	7.81	[6.23]

[a]GB (Greatest Breadth); GL (Greatest Length); BFcr (Greatest Breadth of Cranial Articular Surface); BFcd (Greatest Breadth of Caudal Articular Surface); GLF (Greatest Length from Cranial Articular Surface to Caudal Articular Surface); H (Height) (after von den Driesch 1976).

[b]Left wing broken along midline of dorsal and ventral arches.

[c]Major portion of left wing and part of caudal articular surface missing.

[d]Major portion of right wing and part of ventral arch missing.

[e]Dorsal arch cracked along line of fusion.

[f]Cranial fragment of right wing with alar foramen; this atlas is distinct from and larger than Q-4/1.

[g]Fragments of right wing with alar foramen; also fragments of ventral arch and left cranial articular surface.

Table 19. Axis

Prov.	Port.	But.	Fus.(Cd)	[a]LCDe	[a]LAPa	[a]BFcr	[a]BPacd	[a]BPtr	[a]SBV	[a]BFcd	[a]H
E-10/12	[b]V	[c](1)	---	---	---	---	---	---	---	---	---
F-9/17	C	0	1	10.80	[8.28]	9.80	6.88	[8.80]	5.88	4.72	12.00
F-9/54	C	0	1	10.11	10.15	10.10	7.05	9.88	6.13	4.61	12.55
F-12/2	C	0	1	10.45	9.90	9.39	(7.19)	9.47	6.20	(4.65)	11.90
0-2/11	Da	0	0	11.27	[9.41]	11.23	8.35	[11.78]	7.30	(5.23)	[14.40]
0-3/20	C	0	[d](0.5)	11.92	11.60	11.86	8.62	(12.43)	7.66	(5.60)	(15.50)
P-3/42	Da	(0)	---	[10.03]	[9.77]	(10.92)	---	---	7.17	---	[14.10]
Q-3/11; Q-4/14	V	[c]1	---	---	---	---	---	---	---	---	---

[a]LCDe (Greatest Length of Body); LAPa (Length of Arch including Caudal Articular Process); BFcr (Breadth of Cranial Articular Surface); BPacd (Breadth across Caudal Articular Process); BPtr (Breadth across Transverse Processes); SBV (Smallest Breadth of Vertebra); BFcd (Breadth of Caudal Articular Surface); H (Greatest Height) (after von den Driesch 1976).

[b]From immature individual.

[c]Ventral fragment of dens and cranial articular surface.

[d]Partial separation of caudal pad may be due to weathering rather than to incomplete fusion.

Table 20. Cervical vertebra

Prov.	Port.	But.	Fus. (Cr)	Fus. (Cd)	[a]PL	[b]GLPa	[a]BPacr	[a]BPacd	[a]BPtr	[a]BFcr	[a]HFcr	[a]BFcd	[a]HFcd	[a]H
E-5/1	Pcd	0	---	0	---	---	---	---	---	---	---	---	4.38	---
E-6/23	C	0	0	0	(4.60)	(7.35)	(8.40)	8.00	11.30	3.09	4.76	(5.78)	4.82	[15.90]
E-9/S	Pcd	0	---	0	---	---	---	---	---	---	---	[4.87]	[4.75]	---
E-19/7	Pcd	0	---	0	---	---	---	---	---	---	---	4.68	5.03	---
E-23/1	Pcd	0	---	0	---	---	---	---	---	---	---	---	---	---
E-24/4	Da	0	1	0.5	6.00	8.40	7.70	7.60	9.75	3.53	(4.45)	5.09	4.68	[11.00]
EF-9, 10/S	Pcd	0	---	0	---	---	---	---	---	---	---	---	---	---
EF-11, 14/S	Pcr	0	0	---	---	---	---	---	---	(3.45)	(4.70)	---	---	---
F-8/3	[c]C	0	0	0	(4.25)	7.80	8.65	(7.15)	10.75	3.39	4.14	6.22	4.23	[13.75]
F-8/34B	B,TP	[d]1	1	0.5	5.75	7.35	8.80	8.40	[9.65]	3.36	4.19	(5.04)	4.73	[10.70]
F-9/49	[c]C	0	1	1	5.50	8.15	8.70	7.65	11.45	3.19	4.45	5.99	4.66	24.65
F-9/50	[e]C	0	1	1	6.00	8.00	8.65	8.70	10.50	2.91	4.49	4.68	4.68	17.25
F-9/51	[f]C	0	1	1	6.10	8.45	(8.85)	8.70	[10.00]	3.12	4.50	4.84	4.72	14.10
F-9/52	[g]C	0	1	1	6.30	9.05	8.40	8.50	11.60	3.31	4.25	4.95	4.66	12.80
F-9/53	[h]C	0	1	1	6.30	9.40	7.50	7.80	10.90	3.46	4.29	4.72	4.86	11.15
F-12/1	[c]B,TP	[i]1	1	1	5.10	8.10	8.15	6.70	10.75	3.52	4.48	(6.41)	4.70	[13.95]
F-12/3	[h]C	0	1	1	5.65	9.10	8.05	7.80	[9.35]	3.32	3.78	4.88	4.60	11.05
F-12/4	[g]Da	0	1	1	5.50	7.70	8.30	7.90	[9.35]	3.34	3.86	4.84	4.72	(12.00)
F-12/5	[f]Da	0	1	1	5.35	7.50	8.35	7.75	[8.90]	3.14	4.05	4.76	4.63	(13.20)
F-12/6	[e]C	0	1	1	5.50	7.40	8.30	7.30	10.10	3.02	(3.93)	4.44	4.57	16.45
GH-18/S	[j]Rs	[k](1)	0	0	---	(5.50)	5.40	---	---	2.56	(2.94)	[2.65]	[2.45]	[5.70]
O-2/2	Da	0	0	0	(4.65)	[6.85]	(10.45)	---	[10.50]	(3.45)	(4.48)	(5.68)	[4.59]	[12.10]
O-3/7	Da	0	1	0	(6.40)	[8.25]	10.85	[10.50]	[12.75]	4.01	5.46	(6.17)	(5.76)	(18.65)
O-5/1	[l]B,SPv	(0)	---	---	---	---	---	[7.50]	---	---	---	---	---	---
OP-2, 4/S	[m]B,RTP	(0)	---	1	---	---	---	---	---	---	---	---	(4.63)	---
OP-2, 4/S	Pcd	0	---	0	---	---	---	---	---	---	---	---	---	---
P-2/10	Da	0	0	0	(5.75)	[8.90]	(9.20)	[9.20]	[11.30]	3.64	4.67	(5.32)	5.03	(12.85)
P-3/19	Da	0	0	0.5	(5.35)	8.00	10.05	9.25	[10.60]	3.40	5.18	5.16	(5.75)	[17.20]
P-3/31	Pcd	0	---	0	---	---	---	---	---	---	---	4.64	4.43	---
P-4/5	(Pcd)	0	---	0	---	---	---	---	---	---	---	---	---	---
P-4/22	Da	0	0	0	(3.40)	5.90	6.10	6.25	[6.70]	2.73	3.50	(3.95)	(3.66)	[9.90]
P-4/23	[n]B	1	1	1	6.00	9.45	7.50	8.25	[8.70]	3.49	4.66	5.10	4.77	[9.20]
Q-3/11	Pcd	0	---	0	---	---	---	---	---	---	---	---	---	---
Q-3/21	C	0	0	0	(5.05)	8.65	10.20	9.80	13.20	3.69	4.80	5.79	5.82	(16.85)
Q-4/2	B,TP	[i](1)	0	0	(5.00)	(8.00)	10.15	9.60	11.85	3.29	5.28	5.53	5.45	[14.10]
R-2/2	C	0	1	1	6.30	(8.65)	[10.45]	[9.90]	14.75	4.13	5.11	5.96	5.94	[13.05]

Table 20. (cont.)

---

[a]PL (Length of Body); BPacr (Breadth across Cranial Articular Processes); BPacd (Breadth across Caudal Articular Processes); BPtr (Breadth across Transverse Processes); BFcr (Breadth of Cranial Articular Surface); HFcr (Height of Cranial Articular Surface); BFcd (Breadth of Caudal Articular Surface); HFcd (Height of Caudal Articular Surface); H (Greatest Height) (after von den Driesch 1976).

[b]GLPa (Greatest Length from Cranial to Caudal Articular Processes) (after von den Driesch 1976); values obtained for left and right sides differed significantly; only values for right side listed above.

[c]7th cervical vertebra.

[d]Spinous process and right lateral branch of transverse process missing.

[e]6th cervical vertebra.

[f]5th cervical vertebra.

[g]4th cervical vertebra.

[h]3rd cervical vertebra.

[i]Spinous process missing.

[j]From immature individual.

[k]Specimen damaged during excavation; only partially restored; spinous process, both ventral laminae of transverse processes and one lateral branch of transverse process missing.

[l]Badly weathered; fragment of caudal articular processes and portion of spinous process only.

[m]Badly weathered; caudal half of body and right ventral lamina of transverse process only.

[n]Both transverse processes and spinous process missing.

Table 21. Thoracic vertebra

Prov.	Port.	But.	Fus.(Cr)	Fus.(Cd)	[a]PL	[a]BPtr	[a]BFcr	[a]HFcr	[a]BFcd	[a]HFcd	[a]H
D-1/S	B	[b]1	1	---	[5.30]	---	[4.46]	(4.66)	---	---	---
E-1/6	C	0	1	1	5.23	9.45	4.66	3.81	5.26	3.62	18.35
E-1/7	C	0	1	1	5.48	8.97	4.36	3.74	5.01	3.66	17.72
E-2/1	[c]C	0	1	1	5.40	(7.41)	4.75	(3.39)	(5.55)	(3.37)	15.20
E-2/11	C	0	0	0	(3.75)	8.38	[3.80]	(3.60)	(5.86)	(3.82)	25.20
E-2/16	C	0	1	1	5.60	10.52	5.09	4.28	7.48	(4.62)	33.50
E-7/1	Pcd	0	---	0	---	---	---	---	7.45	4.61	---
E-7/3	Pcd	0	---	0	---	---	---	---	[4.48]	(3.64)	---
E-9/5	Da	0	1	1	5.61	(9.25)	4.70	4.19	6.66	4.43	[25.35]
E-9/6	C	0	1	1	5.60	9.54	4.39	4.15	6.86	4.20	30.20
E-9/7	C	0	1	1	5.60	(9.45)	4.34	4.00	6.53	4.16	33.30
E-9/13	C	0	1	1	5.50	[9.45]	4.61	3.97	6.22	4.06	35.70
E-10/6	[d]C	0	1	1	5.25	8.53	4.30	3.54	5.31	(3.43)	15.51
E-25/1	B,SPv	[e]1	1	1	6.00	[11.31]	5.61	[4.35]	(6.52)	[4.32]	[20.73]
EF-5, 6/S	SPs	0	---	---	---	---	---	---	---	---	---
F-9/4	Da	(0)	0	0	(4.40)	[9.20]	4.17	(3.85)	(5.80)	(3.71)	[29.09]
F-9/12	[h]B,SPv	1	0	0	3.40	[6.53]	(3.44)	(2.80)	4.85	(2.93)	[7.70]
F-9/57	C	0	1	1	5.39	10.88	4.74	4.15	[5.73]	3.98	33.38
F-10/2	Pcr	0	0	---	---	---	(4.29)	(3.74)	---	---	---
F-10/4	Pcd	0	---	0	---	---	---	---	(4.92)	3.92	---
F-22/6	[c]C	0	0	0	(4.91)	9.13	4.93	3.52	5.99	3.44	15.25
F-24/1	B,SPv	[e]1	1	1	5.95	9.10	4.81	(4.13)	6.31	3.97	[9.05]
F-24/2	[f]B,SPv	[e]1	1	1	6.15	11.01	6.19	(3.91)	5.36	4.01	[11.45]
F-24/5	[c]B,SPv	[e]1	1	1	6.00	9.52	5.12	4.04	6.63	3.90	[9.72]
G-8/S	SPv	[g]1	---	---	---	---	---	---	---	---	[9.10]
G-11/3	[h]B	[b]1	0	0	3.30	---	[3.30]	[3.12]	[3.09]	(3.46)	---
G-13/8	SP	[i]1	---	---	---	---	---	---	---	---	[22.60]
G-13/9	C	0	1	1	5.85	10.82	5.23	4.63	7.65	4.80	39.80
G-18/4	C	0	0	0	(4.62)	[9.42]	4.93	3.84	6.61	3.66	22.21
G-21/2	Pcr	0	0	---	---	---	(3.96)	[3.18]	---	---	---
GH-7, 8/S	SPs	0	---	---	---	---	---	---	---	---	---
GH-9, 10/S	[h]SPv	[g]1	---	---	---	---	---	---	---	---	[4.28]
GH-11, 12/S	Pcr	0	0	---	---	---	---	---	---	---	---
H-7/1	Da	0	1	1	5.70	12.55	5.25	4.73	6.81	4.81	[36.85]
H-14/6	Pcd	0	---	0	---	---	---	---	[3.54]	(3.18)	---

Table 21. (cont.)

Prov.	Port.	But.	Fus.(Cr)	Fus.(Cd)	a_{PL}	a_{BPtr}	a_{BFcr}	a_{HFcr}	a_{BFcd}	a_{HFcd}	a_{H}
H-17/13	C	0	1	1	5.30	8.55	4.25	3.79	4.83	3.74	17.70
H-18/6	C	0	1	1	6.20	11.28	5.60	5.53	8.03	5.82	38.90
H-18/7	B,SPv	[e]1	0	0	(5.50)	(7.95)	4.68	(3.98)	(5.48)	(3.68)	[7.60]
H-20/1	C	0	1	1	5.30	8.62	4.07	3.74	5.00	3.55	15.75
H-21/2	C	0	1	1	5.11	9.58	4.70	3.78	(5.35)	(3.56)	19.81
I-16/2	Pcd	0	---	0	---	---	---	---	[5.63]	3.70	---
I-16/3	Pcr	0	0	---	---	---	[4.77]	3.86	---	---	---
I-16/5	B,SPv	[e]1	1	1	5.50	[8.10]	[3.78]	(3.80)	(5.04)	3.69	[10.35]
O-2/9	Pcr	0	0	---	---	---	---	---	---	---	---
O-3/19	B,SPv	[e]1	1	1	6.00	10.63	5.44	4.46	7.68	[4.52]	[16.75]
O-3/36	Da	0	0	0	(5.25)	(9.21)	[4.37]	[3.92]	6.09	3.93	17.13
O-4/6	C	0	(1)	(1)	(5.30)	9.20	4.74	3.85	6.01	3.77	21.65
OP-2, 4/S	SPs	0	---	---	---	---	---	---	---	---	---
OP-2, 4/S	B,SPv	[e](1)	1	1	5.00	[6.90]	[4.07]	3.78	(4.67)	3.66	[9.20]
P-2/5	[h]Da	0	0	0	(2.90)	---	[2.32]	[2.71]	(2.98)	(2.82)	[5.94]
P-2/15	[j]C	0	0.5	0.5	5.65	10.11	4.92	(3.94)	6.22	3.85	17.55
P-2/24	C	0	1	1	5.45	10.36	5.06	(4.40)	7.20	[3.86]	31.35
P-2/31	B	[b]1	(0)	(0)	(4.95)	---	---	---	---	---	---
P-3/3	SPdo	[k](1)	---	---	---	---	---	---	---	---	[10.00]
P-3/29	SPdo	[k]1	---	---	---	---	---	---	---	---	[25.55]
P-3/36	Pcd	0	---	0	---	---	---	---	---	---	---
P-3/37	[d]B,SPv	[e]1	0	0	(3.85)	5.50	3.28	2.95	4.04	2.98	[7.61]
P-3/46	SPs	0	---	---	---	---	---	---	---	---	---
P-3/68	C	0	1	1	5.80	10.79	5.76	5.24	7.48	5.18	28.95
P-3/69	B	[b]1	1	---	---	---	---	---	---	---	---
P-3/71	B,SPv	[e]1	0	0	(4.55)	9.55	4.21	3.76	5.79	3.84	20.20
P-4/15	B,SPv	[e]1	0	0	(4.65)	[8.77]	[3.77]	(3.87)	(6.96)	4.07	[13.50]
P-4/28 & 29	Pcd	0	---	0	---	---	---	---	[4.55]	(4.60)	---
P-4/30	B,SPv	[e]1	0	0	(2.70)	(7.24)	3.81	[2.77]	4.64	(2.98)	[6.84]
Q-1/3	Da	0	(0)	0	[3.90]	[6.69]	---	[2.77]	[4.59]	3.51	[12.90]
Q-2/1	Da	0	1	1	5.85	9.30	5.92	4.95	7.58	5.07	(28.85)
Q-3/10	B,SPv	[e](1)	0	0	(4.50)	[6.13]	[3.39]	3.12	(4.96)	3.07	[5.87]
Q-3/13	C	0	1	1	4.90	[6.20]	4.12	3.27	4.81	[3.12]	16.20
Q-3/19	[c]Da	(0)	1	1	5.80	[9.39]	(5.99)	4.05	[8.17]	(3.75)	[8.82]

Table 21. (cont.)

Prov.	Port.	But.	Fus.(Cr)	Fus.(Cd)	[a]PL	[a]BPtr	[a]BFcr	[a]HFcr	[a]BFcd	[a]HFcd	[a]H
Q-4/10	SP	[i](1)	---	---	---	---	---	---	---	---	[14.80]
Q-4/11	Da	0	0.5	0.5	(4.80)	9.23	5.04	4.08	6.83	3.77	[15.38]
Q-5/1	Da	0	0	0	(5.15)	(9.27)	4.54	(3.79)	(5.95)	[2.68]	[12.80]
Q-6/2	[f]Da	(0)	0	0	(5.30)	(10.29)	(6.03)	(3.72)	5.03	3.65	[14.50]
QR-3, 4/S	SPv	[g](1)	---	---	---	---	---	---	---	---	[8.80]
R-1/1	[j]Da	(0)	[l](0.5)	---	---	---	---	---	---	---	---

[a]PL (Length of Body); BPtr (Breadth across Transverse Processes); BFcr (Breadth of Cranial Articular Surface); HFcr (Height of Cranial Articular Surface); BFcd (Breadth of Caudal Articular Surface); HFcd (Height of Caudal Articular Surface); H (Greatest Height) (after von den Driesch 1976).

[b]Fragment of vertebral body only.

[c]Probable 13th thoracic vertebra.

[d]Probable 12th thoracic vertebra.

[e]Spinous process butchered off.

[f]Probable 14th thoracic vertebra.

[g]Portion of arch and ventral fragment of spinous process only.

[h]From immature individual.

[i]Complete spinous process including portion of arch.

[j]Probable 12th or 13th thoracic vertebra.

[k]Dorsal portion of spinous process only.

[l]Specimen damaged during excavation; badly weathered; partial separation of cranial pad from body of vertebra may be due to damage and weathering rather than to incomplete fusion.

Table 22. Lumbar vertebra

Prov.	Port.	But.	Fus.(Cr)	Fus.(Cd)	^{a}PL	^{a}BPtr	^{a}BFcr	^{a}HFcr	^{a}BFcd	^{a}HFcd	^{a}H
CC-0035/2	B,SP	[b]1	0	0	(5.60)	[9.55]	4.30	(3.75)	5.04	3.63	(13.35)
E-2/17	C	0	0	0	(5.70)	(26.70)	4.40	3.59	5.64	3.49	12.60
E-2/20	B	[c]1	1	1	6.35	[8.70]	4.98	3.69	(6.44)	(3.58)	[8.70]
E-3/15	Pcd	0	---	0	---	---	---	---	6.72	3.65	---
E-19/4 & 6	B,SP	[d]1	0	0	(6.00)	[17.10]	5.37	4.01	6.94	3.47	13.80
EF-1, 2/S	SPdo	[e]1	---	---	---	---	---	---	---	---	---
F-2/4	C	0	0.5	0	(5.75)	[25.65]	4.98	3.83	6.57	3.81	13.30
F-3/7	SPdo	[e]1	---	---	---	---	---	---	---	---	---
F-4/1	B,SP	[f]1	1	1	5.85	[15.40]	4.31	3.61	5.67	3.48	[12.20]
F-9/15	B	[c]1	1	0	(5.35)	[10.45]	(4.50)	3.71	(6.07)	3.39	[8.45]
F-9/37	C	0	0	0	4.85	[16.15]	3.53	3.18	4.03	3.03	11.70
F-11/4	SPdo	[e]1	---	---	---	---	---	---	---	---	---
F-19/2	B	[c]1	0	0	[4.90]	---	---	---	---	---	---
F-24/8	B	[c]1	0	0	5.65	[6.05]	3.80	3.55	4.40	3.47	[9.50]
F-24/9	RTP	[g]1	---	---	---	---	---	---	---	---	---
F-24/10	RTP	[g]1	---	---	---	---	---	---	---	---	---
F-24/11	TP	[g]1	---	---	---	---	---	---	---	---	---
F-24/12	SPdo	[e]1	---	---	---	---	---	---	---	---	---
F-24/13	SPdo	[e]1	---	---	---	---	---	---	---	---	---
F-24/15A	LTP	[g]1	---	---	---	---	---	---	---	---	---
F-24/15B	LTP	[g]1	---	---	---	---	---	---	---	---	---
H-15/2	B,Da	(0)	1	1	5.25	[8.55]	4.58	(2.84)	(5.75)	2.89	---
H-21/7	C	[h]1	0	0	(5.05)	[7.55]	(3.60)	(3.16)	4.52	3.59	12.70
0-2/2	Da	0	0	0	(5.80)	[7.20]	4.69	4.05	4.81	4.00	15.75
0-3/11	C	0	1	1	5.40	18.95	3.94	3.68	4.23	3.48	13.70
0-4/18	Da	0	1	1	6.00	[25.95]	5.38	3.91	7.22	3.65	[12.95]
0-4/19	B,LTP	[i]1	0	0	(5.15)	[11.00]	(3.60)	(3.32)	4.04	3.47	[8.60]
P-2/3	B,TP	[j]1	0	0	(6.05)	[15.10]	(4.95)	(3.77)	(4.75)	(3.78)	[9.30]
P-3/9	[k]Da	0	1	1	2.70	[2.85]	2.45	1.48	2.44	(1.34)	(4.35)
P-3/30	C	0	1	1	6.00	(30.40)	4.67	3.71	6.01	3.51	11.85
P-3/32	[l]Da	0	---	1	[5.80]	[21.95]	[5.10]	[3.48]	(7.24)	[3.16]	[13.80]
P-3/33	[l]Da	0	0	0	---	---	---	---	---	---	---
P-3/44	C	0	0	0	6.20	(30.05)	4.63	3.96	5.81	3.87	[13.05]
Q-3/1	B	[c]1	0	0	(5.80)	---	(4.19)	(3.62)	(4.93)	(3.31)	---

Table 22. (cont.)

[a]PL (Length of Body); BPtr (Breadth across Transverse Processes); BFcr (Breadth of Cranial Articular Surface); HFcr (Height of Cranial Articular Surface); BFcd (Breadth of Caudal Articular Surface); HFcd (Height of Caudal Articular Surface); H (Greatest Height) (after von den Driesch 1976).

[b]Both transverse processes missing; spinous process broken off but restored.

[c]Both transverse processes and spinous process missing.

[d]Left transverse process and tip of right transverse process missing.

[e]Dorsal section of spinous process only.

[f]Both transverse processes and caudal articular processes missing.

[g]Unrestorable butchered transverse process only.

[h]Tip of left transverse process missing.

[i]Right transverse process, tip of left transverse process and entire spinous process missing.

[j]Tips of both transverse processes and entire spinous process missing.

[k]Non-bison.

[l]Badly weathered and corroded.

Table 23. Sacrum

Prov.	Port.	But.	Fus.(Cr)	Fus.(Cd)	Fus.(Msc)	Fus.(Lsc)	[a]GL	[a]PL	[a]GB	[a]BFcr	[a]HFcr
E-3/8	C	0	0.5	0	0	0.5	26.00	24.80	21.15	7.09	3.34
G-12/2	Cr	[b]1	1	---	---	---	---	---	[14.31]	8.32	(3.33)

[a]GL (Greatest Length); PL (Combined Length of Bodies); GB (Greatest Breadth); BFcr (Breadth of Cranial Articular Surface); HFcr (Height of Cranial Articular Surface) (after von den Driesch 1976).

[b]Cranial portion of first sacral vertebra only; specimen cleaved from sacrum along relatively flat plane passing through base of arch and pelvic sacral foramina of vertebra.

Table 24. Caudal vertebra

Prov.	Port.	But.	Fus.(Cr)	Fus.(Cd)	[a]PL	[a]BPtr	[a]BFcr	[a]HFcr	[a]BFcd	[a]HFcd	[a]H
E-2/23	[b]C	0	1	1	3.70	(2.74)	1.44	1.81	1.64	1.57	2.62
E-2/24	[c]C	0	0	0	(4.15)	[7.25]	2.49	1.38	(2.87)	(1.03)	4.26
E-23/2	[c]Da	0	1	---	---	[3.81]	1.85	1.87	---	---	3.04
E-23/3	[c]C	0	1	1	(4.30)	[5.40]	2.05	(1.42)	1.90	1.72	3.40
EF-7, 8/SA	[d]C	0	1	1	1.25	---	0.50	0.52	0.44	0.45	---
EF-7, 8/SB	[d]C	0	1	1	1.80	---	0.70	0.86	0.66	0.66	---
EF-7, 8/SC	[d]C	0	1	1	2.20	---	0.81	0.96	0.74	0.84	---
EF-13, 14/S	[b]C	0	1	1	3.00	(2.31)	1.21	1.34	1.20	1.20	1.75
F-9/10	[c]Da	0	---	1	---	(4.01)	---	---	1.70	1.41	---
F-9/11	[c]Da	0	(0)	0.5	[4.00]	[6.20]	1.90	1.24	(2.31)	(1.23)	(2.90)
F-9/12	[c]Da	0	(0)	---	[3.70]	[4.30]	1.60	(1.57)	---	---	(2.50)
G-11/6	[c]C	0	1	1	4.50	(9.46)	2.76	1.15	2.52	1.61	4.38
GH-18, 22/S	[d]C	0	0	0	(1.95)	---	0.92	0.99	1.02	0.81	---
H-12/1	[d]C	0	1	1	2.25	---	0.71	0.81	0.77	0.85	---
OP-2, 4/S	[b]Do	[e](1)	0	0	---	---	(1.09)	---	---	---	---
P-3/76	[c]Da	0	0	(0)	[3.85]	[4.92]	1.75	1.85	(2.18)	(1.50)	3.07
Q-3/6	[c]Da	0	1	1	4.70	[6.20]	(3.04)	(1.30)	2.75	1.76	---
Q-3/22	[c]Da	0	1	---	[3.00]	[9.20]	2.34	1.13	(2.37)	(1.26)	(2.94)

[a]PL (Length of Body); BPtr (Breadth across Transverse Processes); BFcr (Breadth of Cranial Articular Surface); HFcr (Height of Cranial Articular Surface); BFcd (Breadth of Caudal Articular Surface); HFcd (Height of Caudal Articular Surface); H (Greatest Height) (after von den Driesch 1976).

[b]From middle one-third of caudal vertebral series.

[c]From cranial one-third of caudal vertebral series.

[d]From caudal one-third of caudal vertebral series.

[e]Dorsal fragment only.

Table 25. [a]Unidentifiable vertebral body

Prov.	[b]PL	But.
E-24/1	[5.26]	(1)
[c]EF-1, 2/S (5/30/77)	1.30	0
[c]EF-9, 10/S (6/26/77)	1.20	0
EF-15/S (7/26/77)	---	(1)
EF-16, 22/S (6/27/77)	5.45	(1)
F-4/1	---	(1)
F-25/2	[6.01]	(1)
[c]H-18/9	1.40	0
0-2/1	[4.51]	(1)
0-3/23	[3.72]	(1)
Q-3/10	[5.10]	(1)

[a]Fragmentary vertebral bodies of unknown type that have had their arches, spinous and transverse processes removed.

[b]PL (Length of Body) (after von den Driesch 1976).

[c]Unfused disc-like vertebral body from immature individual.

Table 26. Unidentifiable vertebral pad

Prov.	Port.	[a]BFcr	[a]HFcr	[a]BFcd	[a]HFcd
E-1/12	Pcd	---	---	4.75	3.94
E-19/S (6/28/77)	[b]Pcd	---	---	1.70	1.57
EF/Bkdt	Pcd	---	---	---	---
EF-1, 2/S (5/30/77)	Pcd	---	---	---	---
EF-3, 4/S (5/30/77)	Pcd	---	---	---	---
EF-3, 4/S (5/30/77) (Z=98)	Pcd	---	---	5.57	3.55
EF-5, 6/S (6/6/77)	Pcd	---	---	---	---
EF-9, 10/S (6/10/77) (Z=250)	Pcd	---	---	---	---
EF-9, 10/S (6/13/77)	Pcd	---	---	---	---
EF-9, 10/S (6/13/77)	Pcr	---	---	---	---
EF-9, 10/S (6/16/77)	Pcr	---	---	---	---
EF-15/S (7/30/77)	Pcd	---	---	[3.63]	3.22
EF-17, 18/S (6/26/77)	Pcd	---	---	---	---
EF-21, 22/S (7/18/77)	Pcd	---	---	4.07	3.34
F-9/16	Pcd	---	---	---	---
F-10/2	Pcd	---	---	---	---
F-10/23	Pcd	---	---	4.93	3.99
F-24/6	Pcr	---	---	---	---
G-10/3A	Pcr	3.81	(3.15)	---	---
G-10/3B	Pcd	---	---	4.25	3.22
G-11/3A	Pcr	---	---	---	---
G-11/3B	Pcd	---	---	---	---
G-17/1	Pcr	---	(3.54)	---	---
GH-11, 12/S (7/16/77)	Pcd	---	---	---	---
GH-13, 14/S (7/16/77)	Pcr	---	---	---	---
GH-15/Blk (7/29/77)	Pcr	---	---	---	---
GH-16/Blk (7/18/77)	Pcr	---	---	---	---
GH-18/S (7/9/77)	Pcr	---	---	---	---
GH-19, 22/S (7/23/77)	Pcd	---	---	---	---
H-2/7	Pcr	4.24	4.04	---	---
H-12/S (7/17/77)	Pcd	---	---	---	---
H-17/3	Pcr	[4.38]	4.57	---	---
I-5/1	Pcd	---	---	---	---
I-16/1	Pcr	---	---	---	---
0-4/10	Pcd	---	---	5.14	3.94

Table 26. (cont.)

Prov.	Port.	[a]BFcr	[a]HFcr	[a]BFcd	[a]HFcd
OP-2, 4/S (8/11/77)	Pcd	---	---	---	---
OP-2, 4/S (8/11/77)	Pcd	---	---	---	---
P-3/10	Pcr	---	---	---	---
P-3, 4/S½/S (6/11/77)	Pcd	---	---	---	---
P-3, 4/S½/S (6/12/77)	Pcr	---	---	---	---
P-4/28 (Assoc.)	Pcd	---	---	[7.25]	4.13
Q-4/S (6/6/77)	Pcr	---	---	---	---
QR-001, 002/S (6/13/77)	Pcd	---	---	---	---

[a]BFcr (Breadth of Cranial Articular Surface); HFcr (Height of Cranial Articular Surface); BFcd (Breadth of Caudal Articular Surface); HFcd (Height of Caudal Articular Surface) (after von den Driesch 1976).

[b]From immature individual.

Table 27. [a]Unfused vertebral summit

Prov.	No.
EF-1, 2/S (5/30/77)	3
EF-7, 8/S (6/5/77)	1
G-5, 6/S (6/4/77)	1
GH-15/S (7/29/77)	1
GH-19, 20/S (8/3/77)	1
H-14/13	1
H-17/10	1
OP-2, 4/S (8/9/77)	1
P-4/9	1
Q-4/S (6/6/77)	1

[a]Unfused summits of vertebral transverse and spinous processes; vertebral type unknown.

Table 28. [a]Rib

Prov.	Side	Port.	But.	Fus.	[b]GL	[b]GLht
B-2/2	(L)	Do	1	0	---	---
D-2/1	R	Ms	1	1	[34.80]	---
E-1/1 & 2	R	Da	1	0.5	(56.00)	---
E-1/3	L	C	0	1	40.35	3.07
E-1/4	R	C	0	(0)	51.75	(7.38)
E-1/13 & 14	L	C	0	1	40.30	6.30
E-2/2	L	Ms,V	1	---	[47.70]	---
E-3/1	R	[c]Da	0	1	(28.60)	---
E-3/5	L	Da	0	1	[38.45]	---
E-4/9	R	Do	1	1	[8.99]	4.17
E-4/10	L	Do	1	1	[13.06]	[4.76]
E-8/7	R	C	0	1	38.70	3.19
E-8/8	R	C	0	1	48.25	4.54
E-8/9	R	Da	0	1	[43.90]	[2.75]
E-8/10	R	C	0	1	50.50	4.63
E-8/11 & 23	R	C	1	1	52.70	4.77
E-8/12	R	Da	0	1	[52.50]	---
E-8/14	R	C	0	1	31.30	4.86
E-8/15	L	Da	0	0	[40.00]	4.60
E-8/25	R	C	0	1	53.35	6.09
E-8/26	R	C	0	1	50.80	6.19
E-9/4	R	Da	0	1	[45.80]	6.46
E-9/8	L	C	0	1	43.40	6.23
E-9/9	L	C	0	1	(38.55)	(5.06)
E-9/18	R	C	0	1	43.30	6.28
E-10/1	R	Ms,V	1	---	[50.30]	---
E-11/1	L	C	0	1	38.10	(4.11)
E-18/1	L	C	0	1	34.65	5.78
E-19/3	L	Da	0	1	[30.20]	5.81
E-19/9	L	Do	1	1	[11.27]	6.01
E-23/6	---	Do	1	1	[5.70]	[4.87]
F-0024/7	R	Do	1	1	[22.80]	(5.17)
F-0024/11	R	Ms,Do	1	(1)	[22.00]	6.18
F-1/A	R	Ms,Do	1	1	[20.80]	7.37

Table 28. (cont.)

Prov.	Side	Port.	But.	Fus.	[b]GL	[b]GLht
F-2/1	R	Ms,V	1	---	[36.10]	---
F-3/1	R	C	0	1	35.70	6.06
F-7/1	R	Da	0	---	[33.20]	---
F-8/28	L	Ms,V	1	---	[48.90]	---
F-9/14	L	C	0	1	46.75	4.60
F-9/38	R	Da	0	1	[50.00]	6.21
F-9/45	L	C	0	1	36.10	5.11
F-9/46	L	C	0	1	31.25	4.61
F-9/47	L	[c]C	0	1	27.70	4.86
F-9/58	R	C	0	1	38.65	5.67
F-9/59	R	C	0	1	35.45	5.12
F-9/60	R	C	0	1	31.95	4.68
F-9/61	R	[c]C	0	1	27.40	4.87
F-10/17	L	C	0	1	57.35	5.68
F-10/19	R	Da	0	1	[49.75]	4.94
F-10/20	L	Da	0	1	[42.55]	4.25
F-16/1	R	[c]C	0	(0)	26.95	(4.42)
F-16/2	R	Do	1	(0)	[16.20]	4.71
F-16/5	R	Ms,Do	1	1	[45.85]	[2.93]
F-24/5	R	C	0	1	58.00	7.58
G-11/5	L	C	0	1	43.80	6.78
G-11/11	L	Da	0	1	[49.50]	6.12
G-14/1	L	Do	1	1	[8.73]	(7.30)
G-16/1	R	Ms,Do	1	1	[23.15]	4.97
G-18/2	R	Da	0	---	[37.00]	---
G-19/7	R	Ms,Do	1	1	[36.50]	5.62
GH-19, 22/S	(L)	Do	(1)	1	---	---
H-12/3	(R)	Do	1	1	[5.60]	---
H-14/5	L	Da	0	1	[45.15]	---
H-14/11	R	Da	0	1	(51.60)	[3.42]
H-16/3	R	C	0	1	48.35	7.35
H-17/2	R	Ms,V	1	---	[48.70]	---
H-17/5A	L	[c]C	0	0	26.90	4.75
H-17/5B & 8	R	[d]Da	0	---	[23.00]	---

Table 28. (cont.)

Prov.	Side	Port.	But.	Fus.	[b]GL	[b]GLht
H-17/14	L	C	0	1	52.10	5.73
H-17/17	R	C	0	1	29.10	4.70
H-21/4	L	Do	1	1	[6.02]	5.67
0-2/7	R	Do	1	0	[9.50]	(5.91)
0-3/6 & 12	L	C	0	1	(36.50)	5.46
0-3/26	R	Ms,Do	1	0	[11.20]	(4.40)
0-4/12	L	Do	1	1	[8.53]	4.31
P-3/40	R	C	0	1	35.00	5.86
P-3/63	L	Do	1	0	[16.50]	(4.28)
P-3/72	L	Ms,Do	1	1	[28.80]	4.55
P-4/1	L	Do	1	(1)	[6.15]	(6.70)
P-4/8 & 11	R	Da	0	1	[36.00]	(5.93)
P-4/13	R	Da	0	1	[32.50]	5.16
P-4/14	---	Do	1	1	---	---
Q-4/8	L	Ms,Do	1	1	[18.10]	(6.40)
Q-4/19	L	Do	1	1	---	---
Q-5/1	---	Do	1	1	---	---

[a]Each entry may be treated as a different rib when determining minimum number of individuals.
[b]GL (Greatest Length); GLht (Greatest Length between Head and Tubercle).
[c]Cranial rib with greatly enlarged ventral portion of blade.
[d]From immature individual.

Table 29. [a]Miscellaneous rib-vertebral process fragments

Prov.	No.	Wt.(g)	Comments
AB-1, 2/S (Z=104)	1	1.8	
C-1/S (Z=128)	1	1.7	[b]RB
C-2/S (Z=128)	1	0.9	
D-2/1	1	57.0	RB
D-3/2	1	3.2	
D-10/1A	1	6.2	RB
D-11, 12/S (7/11/77)	6	4.6	
D-12/S (7/10/77)	1	1.2	
E-1/S (5/28/77)	1	1.3	
E-3/3	1	2.6	
E-3/11	1	13.4	
E-3, 4/S (6/4/77)	7	4.7	
E-3, 4/S (6/5/77)	6	3.1	
E-4/5	1	3.6	
E-4/6	1	2.3	
E-5/1	1	1.6	
E-5, 6/S (6/7/77)	10	13.2	
E-6/4	1	1.1	
E-6/5	1	24.8	RB
E-7/2	1	27.0	RB
E-8/3	1	13.5	RB
E-9/5	1	11.0	[c]RS
E-10/S (6/14/77)	2	4.0	
E-11/S (6/27/77)	1	1.9	
E-18/12	1	0.6	[d]RT
E-22/5	1	36.1	RB
E-26/3	1	9.5	RB
EF/Bkdt	3	77.7	3RB
EF/Bkdt (6/27/77)	1	1.9	
EF-1, 2/S (5/29/77)	1	0.8	
EF-1, 2/S (5/30/77)	19	14.5	
EF-1, 2/S (5/31/77)	9	11.8	
EF-3, 4/S (5/30/77)	4	3.7	
EF-3, 4/S (6/5/77)	1	0.4	

Table 29. (cont.)

Prov.	No.	Wt.(g)	Comments
EF-4/S	9	14.3	1RB; 1^{e}RH
EF-5, 6/S (6/5/77)	1	1.5	
EF-5, 6/S (6/6/77)	6	24.1	1RB
EF-5, 6/S (Z=98)	4	20.9	1RB
EF-7, 8/S (5/31/77)	1	0.8	
EF-7, 8/S (6/5/77)	5	4.7	
EF-7, 8/S (6/6/77)	15	15.2	1RT
EF-8/S (6/5/77)	2	3.2	
EF-9, 10/S (6/10/77)	2	1.4	
EF-9, 10/S (6/12/77)	6	6.2	
EF-9, 10/S (6/13/77)	14	9.9	
EF-9, 10/S (6/14/77)	17	15.2	
EF-9, 10/S (6/16/77)	18	16.7	
EF-9, 10/S (6/26/77)	1	1.0	
EF-11/S (Blk) (6/28/77)	13	13.8	1RB
EF-11/S (7/1/77)	4	5.5	
EF-11, 12/S (6/26/77)	3	3.0	
EF-11, 14/S (6/14/77)	3	10.4	1RS; 1 waterworn
EF-11, 14/S (6/15/77)	10	8.4	
EF-15/Blk (7/30/77)	3	4.2	1RH
EF-16, 18/S (6/27/77)	1	2.4	
EF-17, 18/S (6/26/77)	11	26.2	
EF-21, 22/S (7/18/77)	1	1.6	
EF-22/S (7/25/77)	1	6.2	
EF-22/S (7/26/77)	2	9.7	1 with sharp cut
EF-22/S (7/29/77)	1	1.1	
EF-23, 26/S (7/23/77)	2	3.5	1RB
EF-23, 26/S (7/25/77)	2	4.2	1RH
EF-25, 26/S (7/18/77)	4	4.4	
F-0024/2	1	46.5	RB
F-0024/10	1	100.1	RB; RS
F-0024/12	1	1.4	
F-0024/S	5	7.1	Screening of talus
F-1, 2/Lower Gravel	2	3.7	

Table 29. (cont.)

Prov.	No.	Wt.(g)	Comments
F-2/S (Z=122)	1	4.5	
F-3/S (6/3/77)	6	6.3	1 waterworn
F-3/2	1	30.6	RB
F-3/4	1	3.1	
F-3/6	1	1.1	
F-4/5	1	2.7	
F-5/S (5/30/77) (Z=98)	1	2.2	
F-7/1	1	0.9	
F-8/22	1	23.5	RB
F-9/2	1	6.2	
F-9/14	1	1.0	
F-9/33	1	46.2	RB
F-9/38	1	9.1	
F-9/44	3	3.0	
F-10/S (6/14/77)	1	0.5	
F-10/7	1	3.7	RH
F-10/21	1	26.8	RS
F-10/22	1	3.5	
F-10/29	1	3.2	
F-11/3	1	3.8	
F-11/5	1	1.6	
F-11/6	1	3.3	
F-14, 15/S (6/27/77)	2	5.0	
F-16/1	1	1.2	*f* RHs
F-16/3	1	39.4	RB
F-16/6	1	2.0	
F-18/1	1	94.8	RB
F-22/7	1	22.6	RB
F-22/10	1	26.0	RB
F-24/5	1	2.0	
G-5, 6/S (6/4/77)	5	13.1	
G-6/1	1	3.7	
G-7/1	1	2.9	
G-7/2	1	3.3	
G-7/3	1	1.9	

Table 29. (cont.)

Prov.	No.	Wt.(g)	Comments
G-9/2	1	8.5	RS
G-11/2	1	6.6	RB
G-11, 12/S (7/17/77)	2	0.7	
G-12/1	1	14.2	RB
G-12/5	1	16.9	RS
G-13/S (7/10/77)	1	1.0	RHs
G-13/6	1	12.8	RS
G-13/10	1	4.0	
G-15/2	1	1.3	RHs
G-16/6	1	1.4	
G-16/7	1	1.4	
G-19/3	1	5.5	
G-19/4	1	3.0	
G-20/2	1	21.4	RS; cranial-type rib
G-20/3	1	1.0	
G-21, 22/S (8/3/77)	2	1.2	
G-22/1	1	2.4	RB
GH-7, 8/S (6/4/77)	2	4.8	
GH-11, 12/S (7/12/77)	5	5.8	1RHs
GH-11, 12/S (7/16/77)	3	6.6	
GH-13, 14/S (7/11/77)	7	15.4	
GH-13, 14/S (7/12/77)	8	4.4	2 burned
GH-13, 14/S (7/15/77)	4	6.3	
GH-14, 15/S (7/9/77)	3	6.0	
GH-15/Blk (7/29/77)	4	3.2	
GH-16/S (7/4/77)	11	17.6	1RS; 1RH
GH-16/Blk (7/19/77)	3	3.1	
GH-16, 18/S (7/12/77)	3	1.4	
GH-16, 19/S (7/5/77)	7	9.9	1RH
GH-17/S (7/9/77)	10	8.6	
GH-18/S (7/9/77)	4	7.0	
GH-19, 20/S (8/3/77)	2	1.6	
GH-19, 22/S (7/23/77)	4	2.7	
GH-19, 22/S (7/25/77)	2	1.4	
GH-19, 22/S (7/26/77)	4	4.0	

Table 29. (cont.)

Prov.	No.	Wt.(g)	Comments
H-2/1	2	6.2	
H-5/S (7/22/77)	1	1.0	RH
H-9, 10/S$\frac{1}{2}$/S (6/14/77)	1	1.0	
H-11, 12/S (7/3/77)	1	2.4	
H-12/S (7/17/77)	2	4.9	
H-16/S (S. Wall) (7/11/77)	3	6.0	
H-16/14	1	6.1	RB
H-16, 18/S (7/11/77)	6	11.2	
H-16, 18/S (7/16/77)	2	2.7	
H-17/16	1	1.7	
H-19/2	1	9.1	RS
H-19/3	1	7.1	
H-19/4	1	2.0	
O-2/6	1	13.0	RS
O-3/14	1	1.6	
O-3/28	1	0.8	
O-3/32	1	6.0	
O-4/15	2	2.3	
O-4/20	1	0.8	
OP-2, 4/S (7/30/77)	9	9.3	
OP-2, 4/S (8/1/77)	18	11.1	1[g]RS; 1RHs; 1RT
OP-2, 4/S (8/4/77)	19	20.3	2[g]RS; 2RH
OP-2, 4/S (8/5/77)	26	19.0	2[g]RS
OP-2, 4/S (8/8/77)	3	4.0	
OP-2, 4/S (8/9/77)	2	1.7	
OP-2, 4/S (8/10/77)	8	9.1	
OP-2, 4/S (8/11/77)	1	2.5	
P-2/9	1	3.4	RB
P-2/26	1	1.5	
P-2/30	1	2.5	
P-3/S (6/13/77)	3	4.1	
P-3/12	1	14.7	RB
P-3/17	1	8.7	RB
P-3/20	1	5.7	
P-3/26	1	3.0	

Table 29. (cont.)

Prov.	No.	Wt. (g)	Comments
P-3/28	2	7.3	RB
P-3/66	1	2.3	
P-3/69	1	4.7	RT
P-3/79	1	1.0	
P-3, 4/S½/S (6/11/77)	6	6.2	1[g]RB
P-3, 4/S½/S (6/12/77)	10	10.6	
P-4/6	1	6.2	RB
P-4/8	1	1.2	
P-4/15	1	0.5	
Q-1/2	1	8.1	[h]T
Q-2/2	1	3.4	T
Q-3/S (6/6/77)	2	0.5	
Q-3/6	1	0.4	
Q-3/20	1	10.9	RS
Q-4/S (6/10/77)	2	1.4	
Q-4/3	1	1.6	
Q-4/27	1	2.1	
Q-4/28	1	0.7	[g]RB
Q-4/35	1	8.1	
Q-5/1	2	2.7	
Q-6/1	1	12.5	RS
QR-1, 2/S (6/6/77)	1	2.0	RH
QR-3, 4/S (6/4/77)	2	1.7	

[a]Fragments of ribs not to be included in computation of minimum number of individuals; also fragments of ribs and vertebral processes with one or more old breaks (butchering debris); some of these fragments undoubtedly represent natural disintegration products.

[b]Fragment of rib blade or midsection.

[c]Fragment of sternal extremity of rib.

[d]Rib tubercle fragment.

[e]Rib head fragment.

[f]Unfused cap (epiphysis) of rib head.

[g]From immature individual.

[h]Possible fragment of thoracic spinous process.

Table 30. [a]Costal cartilage.

Prov.	[b]GL	[b]GB
D-11,12/S (7/11/77)	[1.25]	[0.98]
E-3,4/S (6/4/77)	[0.77]	[1.47]
E-8/2	9.35	2.75
E-8/22	[9.96]	1.05
E-9/S (6/14/77)	[11.60]	[0.73]
E-19/2	(22.20)	4.41
E-20/4	[4.58]	2.65
EF-4/S (5/31/77)	[3.50]	[2.20]
EF-5,6/S (6/6/77)	[10.90]	[1.30]
EF-9 (near F-8/30)	[8.50]	2.21
EF-9 (near F-8/30)	[4.15]	[1.89]
EF-9,10/S (6/12/77)	[2.95]	[1.91]
EF-9,10/S (6/26/77)	[4.31]	[0.89]
EF-11/S (7/1/77)	5.87	2.69
EF-23,26/S (7/16/77)	[6.46]	(3.18)
F-8/1	[11.35]	[1.42]
F-8/6 & 30	18.85	3.67
F-8/31	[7.97]	2.21
F-8/32	9.94	2.39
F-8/37A	9.03	2.75
F-8/37B	[5.48]	2.67
F-8/38	8.83	[1.90]
F-8/39	13.10	2.25
F-8/41A	7.10	2.38
F-8/41B	6.76	2.41
F-8/41C	6.84	2.56

Table 30. (cont.)

Prov.	[b]GL	[b]GB
F-8/41D	[7.17]	2.61
F-8/41E	[12.35]	1.38
F-9/48	16.40	2.28
F-10/8	[11.30]	(0.88)
G-12/6	(18.50)	3.23
G-12/S (7/12/77)	[5.96]	[0.93]
GH-11,12/S (7/16/77)	[5.45]	[1.10]
GH-19,22/S (7/15/77)	[10.68]	2.83
GH-19,22/S (7/23/77)	[4.15]	[1.80]
H-10/S (6/26/77)	[3.08]	[1.31]
H-14/9	(18.65)	2.48
H-14/14	[14.65]	1.59
H-16,17/S (7/23/77)	[6.32]	2.60
H-16,17/S (7/23/77)	[8.20]	(1.34)
H-18/17	[14.50]	2.50
H-20/2	(8.95)	3.02
O-3/3	7.20	3.30
O-3/33	10.03	2.91
P-2/8	[12.00]	2.25
P-3/62	21.60	1.58
P-3/77	[3.47]	(2.06)
P-4/4	(5.30)	(2.75)
P-4/12	[5.99]	(2.49)
P-4/17	[3.78]	[1.68]
QR-3,4/S (6/4/77)	[3.09]	[1.43]

[a]All items listed above represent different, non-restorable specimens of costal cartilage.
[b]GL (Greatest Length); GB (Greatest Breadth).

Table 31. Sternebra

Prov.	Comments
E-8/16	3rd or 4th (probable 4th)
F-8/29A	[a] 1st (manubrium)
F-8/29B	2nd
F-8/29C	3rd
F-8/29D	4th
F-8/29E	5th
F-8/29F	6th; fusing to F-9/29G
F-8/29G	7th; fusing to F-9/29F
G-22/7	2nd
G-22/8	5th
GH-7, 8/S	2nd; damaged
GH-19, 22/S	2nd; damaged
GH-19, 22/S	unidentified fragment
H-21/10	1st (manubrium)
H-27/2	3rd, 4th or 5th; weathered
P-3/54	3rd
P-3/65	6th
P-4/25	4th or 5th (probable 5th)
R-2/1	5th or 6th (probable 5th)

[a] Sternebrae from F-8/29 articulated.

Table 32. Scapula

Prov.	Side	Port.	But.	Fus.(SGT)	[a]HS	[a]DHA	[a]Ld	[a]SLC	[a]GLP	[a]LG	[a]BG
A-1/1	---	Bl	[b]1	---	---	---	---	---	---	---	---
A-2/3	L	Cd	[c]1	---	---	---	---	---	---	---	---
A-2/4(2 pieces)	---	Bl	[b]1	---	---	---	---	---	---	---	---
A-2/5	L	Cd	[c]1	---	---	---	---	---	---	---	---
C-1/S (Z=128)	---	Bl	[b]1	---	---	---	---	---	---	---	---
D-10/1B	---	Bl	[b]1	---	---	---	---	---	---	---	---
D-11,12/S (7/11/77)	---	Bl	[b]1	---	---	---	---	---	---	---	---
E-4/3	L	CB	[d]1	1	[36.60]	---	---	5.69	7.14	6.26	4.46
E-8/5	L	C	0	1	50.25	47.70	(26.00)	7.70	9.65	7.75	6.20
E-10/1	---	Bo	[e]1	---	---	---	---	---	---	---	---
E-10/4	---	Bl	[b]1	---	---	---	---	---	---	---	---
E-12/2	---	Bl	[b]1	---	---	---	---	---	---	---	---
E-24/5	L	CB	[d]1	1	[30.15]	[28.90]	[12.61]	6.12	7.58	6.25	4.96
EF-11/S (6/28/77)	---	P	[f]1	---	---	---	---	---	---	---	---
EF-11,14/S (6/15/77)	---	Bl	[b]1	---	---	---	---	---	---	---	---
EF-13,14/S (6/26/77)	---	Bl	[b]1	---	---	---	---	---	---	---	---
F-0024/8	R	C	0	1	(45.10)	[44.30]	[19.80]	6.45	7.97	6.92	(5.32)
F-1/6	R	Cd	[c]1	---	---	---	---	---	---	---	---
F-4/8	---	P	[f]1	---	---	---	---	---	---	---	---
F-4/S (5/30/77)	---	Bl	[b]1	---	---	---	---	---	---	---	---
F-9/36	R	[g]C	0	1	41.60	41.60	21.10	6.57	7.68	6.42	5.23
F-10/8	L	[g]C	0	1	41.40	41.50	20.90	6.58	7.54	6.45	5.17
G-5,6/S (6/4/77)	---	Bl	[b]1	---	---	---	---	---	---	---	---
GH-16/Blk (7/18/77)	L	D	[h]1	(1)	---	---	---	---	---	(7.13)	(5.35)
GH-16,18/S (7/18/77)	(L)	Spn	[i]1	---	---	---	---	---	---	---	---
GH-16,18/S (7/18/77)	(L)	Cd	[j]1	---	---	---	---	---	---	---	---
H-2/1	---	Bo	[e]1	---	---	---	---	---	---	---	---
H-9,10/S½/S(6/14/77)	---	Bl	[b]1	---	---	---	---	---	---	---	---
H-16/6	---	Bl	[b]1	---	---	---	---	---	---	---	---
H-16/8	L	Spn	[k]1	---	---	---	---	---	---	---	---
H-16,18/S (7/11/77)	---	Bl	[b]1	---	---	---	---	---	---	---	---
H-16,18/S (7/11/77)	---	Bl	[b]1	---	---	---	---	---	---	---	---
H-17/12	---	Bl	[b]1	---	---	---	---	---	---	---	---
H-18/12	---	[l]P	---	---	---	---	---	---	---	---	---

Table 32. (cont.)

Prov.	Side	Port.	But.	Fus.(SGT)	[a]HS	[a]DHA	[a]Ld	[a]SLC	[a]GLP	[a]LG	[a]BG
O-3/1	R	D	[m]1	1	---	---	---	7.77	9.05	(7.37)	6.37
O-3/15	---	Bl	[b]1	---	---	---	---	---	---	---	---
O-3/38	R	[n]Da	(0)	(0)	[8.59]	[9.64]	[5.76]	2.27	---	(2.92)	(1.50)
O-4/18	---	Bl	[b]1	---	---	---	---	---	---	---	---
OP-2,4/S (8/4/77)	---	P	[f]1	---	---	---	---	---	---	---	---
OP-2,4/S (8/5/77)	---	P	[f]1	---	---	---	---	---	---	---	---
P-2/32	L	Cd	[o]1	---	---	---	---	---	---	---	---
P-3/73	R	Spn	[p]1	---	---	---	---	---	---	---	---
P-3/S (6/13/77)	---	Bl	[b]1	---	---	---	---	---	---	---	---
Q-3/S (6/3/77)	---	Bo	[e]1	---	---	---	---	---	---	---	---
Q-4/7	---	Bl	[b]1	---	---	---	---	---	---	---	---

[a]HS (Height along Spine); DHA (Diagonal Height); Ld (Dorsal Length); SLC (Smallest Length of Neck); GLP (Greatest Length of Glenoid Process); LG (Length of Glenoid Cavity); BG (Breadth of Glenoid Cavity) (after von den Driesch 1976).

[b]Small fragment of blade.

[c]Fragment of caudal border.

[d]Major portion of caudal and cranial blade missing; distal portion of spine including acromion broken off but restored.

[e]Fragment of border; side unknown.

[f]Proximal extremity with portion of border.

[g]Portion of cartilage on proximal border remains intact.

[h]Glenoid cavity and small portion of neck only; fused supraglenoid tubercle missing.

[i]Four partially restorable fragments of spine.

[j]Fragment of caudal angle.

[k]Proximal end of spine.

[l]Fragment of cartilage from proximal extremity.

[m]Distal end with intact glenoid cavity, portion of neck, and butchered fragment of acromion area of spine.

[n]Probable non-bison.

[o]Caudal angle and portion of proximal caudal border.

[p]Major portion of spine.

Table 33. Humerus

Prov.	Side	Port.	But.	Fus.(P)	Fus.(D)	[a]GL	[a]GLC	[a]Bp	[a]SD	[a]Bd	[a]BT
E-2/8	R	C	0	0	1	30.90	27.95	9.65	3.85	7.91	7.68
EF-3,4/S	L	D	[b]1	---	(1)	---	---	---	---	[7.52]	[7.52]
F-9/8	L	C	0	1	1	31.90	28.65	10.55	4.30	8.10	7.90
F-9/27	R	C	0	1	1	32.10	28.66	10.50	4.36	8.28	7.85
F-10/18	R	C	0	1	1	37.71	33.00	12.61	4.94	9.40	9.25
G-22/5	(R)	P	[c](1)	(1)	---	---	---	---	---	---	---
H-15/1	R	D	[d]1	---	1	[26.25]	---	---	4.92	9.25	9.00
O-2/15	R	[e]Rs	---	---	---	---	---	---	---	---	---
O-4/7	L	C	0	1	1	30.20	27.41	9.90	4.13	8.30	(8.12)
[f]O-4/13	L	C	0	1	1	36.55	31.80	10.75	4.53	9.08	8.96
P-2/11	R	[g]P	(1)	1	---	[21.00]	---	12.30	---	---	---
P-3/4	L	P	[h]1	1	---	[17.37]	[15.49]	(10.32)	---	---	---
P-3/35	R	[i]Pe	0	0	---	[6.78]	---	[4.42]	---	---	---
P-3/64	R	[j]Pe	0	0	---	---	---	[12.65]	---	---	---
Q-4/5	(L)	P	[k]1	1	---	---	---	---	---	---	---

[a]GL (Greatest Length); GLC (Greatest Length from Head); Bp (Proximal Breadth); SD (Smallest Breadth of Diaphysis); Bd (Distal Breadth); BT (Greatest Breadth of Trochlea) (after von den Driesch 1976).

[b]Distal condyle only.

[c]Lateral tuberosity only.

[d]Proximal end of humerus from deltoid tuberosity upward is missing; shaft is broken obliquely to form slight posterior-medial projection; small flake-like scars on exterior surface of projection suggest possible use as chopping or defleshing tool; no polish.

[e]Humerus weathered and completely fragmented by exposure in wall of arroyo; partial restoration indicates that specimen probably had not been butchered.

[f]Shaft submitted to Geochron Laboratories, Cambridge, Mass. for radiocarbon analysis (No. GX-5098-A; GX-5098-G).

[g]Shaft broken off irregularly in vicinity of deltoid tuberosity; no evidence for use as tool.

[h]Shaft broken obliquely near deltoid tuberosity to form anterior point; small, flake-like scars on exterior surface of point suggest possible use as chopping or defleshing tool; no polish.

[i]Fragment of unfused epiphyseal lateral tuberosity; not from same individual as P-3/64.

[j]Fragment of unfused epiphyseal head only; not from same individual as P-3/35.

[k]Fragment of head only.

Table 34. Radius

Prov.	Side	Port.	But.	Fus. (P)	Fus. (D)	Assoc. Ulna	[a]GL(RU)	[a]GL	[a]Bp	[a]BFp	[a]SD	[a]Bd	[a]BFd
E-3/16	(R)	P	[b]1	1	---	---	---	[22.45]	[5.94]	[4.17]	---	---	---
E-19/8	(L)	P	[c]1	1	---	---	---	---	---	---	---	---	---
F-0024/12	L	P	0	1	---	F-0024/13	---	[19.50]	8.48	7.91	[4.62]	---	---
F-9/9	L	C	0	1	1	F-9/9	39.35	30.09	8.36	7.88	4.44	7.46	6.95
F-9/26	R	C	0	1	1	F-9/26	39.00	30.05	8.46	7.84	4.40	7.80	7.01
F-16/4	R	P	[d]1	1	---	(F-16/7)	---	[25.22]	8.84	8.06	---	---	---
G-20/1	R	P	[e]1	1	---	---	---	[3.28]	3.80	3.69	---	---	---
H-11/4	L	D	[f]1	---	0	H-11/5	---	[22.38]	---	---	---	[6.10]	(5.88)
H-14/2	R	C	0	1	0	H-14/1	[40.01]	33.50	9.50	8.93	(5.10)	8.35	8.28
0-3/41	R	C	0	1	1	P-4/10	---	33.89	10.15	9.31	5.57	9.46	(8.47)
P-2/25	R	Di	[g]1	---	0	---	---	[24.53]	---	---	[4.76]	[8.14]	---
P-3/38	R	D	[h]1	---	1	P-3/38	---	[27.20]	---	---	4.47	7.50	7.24
Q-4/13	R	C	0	0.5	0	---	---	23.90	6.89	6.68	3.44	6.56	6.36
QR-001,002/S	R	[i]De	---	---	---	---	---	---	---	---	---	[7.25]	(7.25)

[a]GL(RU) (Greatest Length of Articulated Radius and Ulna); GL (Greatest Length); Bp (Proximal Breadth); BFp (Breadth of Proximal Articular Surface); SD (Smallest Breadth of Diaphysis); Bd (Distal Breadth); BFd (Breadth of Distal Articular Surface) (after von den Driesch 1976).

[b]Medial half of proximal end and shaft; distal end missing; distal end slightly pointed suggesting possible use as chopping or defleshing tool; specimen badly weathered.

[c]Lateral half of proximal end; no shaft remaining; specimen weathered.

[d]Proximal end and entire lateral half of shaft; distal end missing; shaft pointed at distal end suggesting possible use as chopping or defleshing tool; no flake-scars or polish on point.

[e]Proximal end only; probable non-bison.

[f]Distal end (unfused) and posterior-lateral half of shaft; styloid process broken off; proximal end of shaft pointed suggesting possible use as chopping or defleshing tool; specimen badly weathered.

[g]Distal portion of diaphysis; distal epiphysis missing; anterior-lateral portion of shaft toward proximal end projects to form a point suggesting use as chopping or defleshing tool; small flake-scars on exterior surface; no polish.

[h]Distal end and shaft; shaft broken obliquely to form medial point suggesting use as chopping or defleshing tool; flake-scars on exterior surface of point; no polish.

[i]Distal epiphysis only; styloid process missing; badly weathered.

Table 35. Ulna

Prov.	Side	Port.	But.	Fus.(P)	Fus.(D)	Assoc. Radius	[a]GL	[a]LO	[a]DPA	[a]SDO	[a]BPC
E-9/19	L	P	[b]1	0	---	---	[9.35]	[8.32]	[4.35]	[4.84]	[2.55]
F-0024/13	L	P	---	1	---	F-0024/12	[28.30]	10.79	7.56	5.68	4.84
F-1/3	---	Ms	[c]1	---	---	---	[7.61]	---	---	---	---
F-9/9	L	C	0	1	1	F-9/9	38.20	(10.43)	7.64	5.59	4.78
F-9/26	R	C	0	1	1	F-9/26	37.31	10.61	7.73	5.52	(4.74)
F-11/1	L	P	[d]1	1	---	---	[22.65]	(12.70)	[8.29]	[5.90]	(4.74)
F-16/7	R	P	[e]1	0	---	(F-16/4)	[20.30]	[10.31]	9.09	6.02	5.18
F-17/2	R	P	[f]1	1	---	---	[13.10]	[8.55]	(7.81)	(5.77)	(4.60)
F-25/1	---	Ms	[c]1	---	---	---	[10.35]	---	---	---	---
H-11/5	L	Ms	[c]1	---	---	H-11/4	[17.80]	---	---	---	---
H-14/1	R	Da	0	---	(0)	H-14/2	[38.80]	[7.98]	8.90	(6.39)	5.60
H-17/6	L	P	[g]1	1	---	---	[14.71]	10.46	8.03	6.92	4.57
P-3/38	R	D	[h]1	---	1	P-3/38	[19.20]	---	---	---	---
P-4/10	R	D	[i]1	---	1	0-3/41	[22.70]	---	---	---	---

[a]GL (Greatest Length); LO (Length of Olecranon); DPA (Depth across Processus Anconaeus); SDO (Smallest Depth of Olecranon); BPC (Breadth across Coronoid Process) (after von den Driesch 1976).

[b]Proximal epiphysis missing; caudal border of olecranon and entire shaft missing.

[c]Ulnar shaft fragment only.

[d]Shaft broken off below coronoid process; proximal tuberosity of olecranon battered.

[e]Proximal epiphysis missing; shaft broken off below coronoid process.

[f]Shaft broken off below coronoid process; proximal tuberosity of olecranon battered.

[g]Shaft broken off at coronoid process.

[h]Shaft broken off well above styloid process; shaft completely fused to body of radius.

[i]Fragment of ulnar shaft that restores to remnant of shaft and styloid process of 0-3/41.

Table 36. Radial carpal

Prov.	Side	Port.	But.	[a]GB	[b]GL
E-10/1	R	C	0	2.66	3.27
F-9/35F	L	C	0	2.86	2.99
F-9/44D	R	C	0	2.80	2.99
F-24/4	R	C	0	(2.82)	(3.10)
H-11/3B	L	C	0	(2.55)	(3.03)
H-16/5	L	C	0	2.90	3.24
P-3/13	R	C	0	(3.09)	3.26
P-3/49	R	C	0	2.85	3.34
Q-3/7	L	Da	0	[2.50]	[3.28]

[a]GB (Greatest Breadth) (after von den Driesch 1976).
[b]GL (Greatest Length).

Table 37. Intermediate carpal

Prov.	Side	Port.	But.	[a]GBp	[a]GD	[a]DL
F-9/11	R	C	0	3.17	3.74	2.78
F-9/35H	L	C	0	3.17	3.80	(2.68)
F-9/44C	R	C	0	3.05	3.90	2.72
G-5,6/S	L	C	0	3.14	4.00	2.65
G-22/3	R	C	0	2.96	3.95	2.57
H-10/1	L	C	0	3.10	3.87	2.71
H-11/3A	L	C	0	3.01	[3.54]	2.65
H-14/4C	R	C	0	3.59	4.52	3.18
H-16,18/S	L	C	0	[2.96]	3.87	2.71
HI-16,19/S	R	Da	0	2.96	[3.94]	2.50
P-3/23	R	C	0	3.35	4.24	2.90
P-3/52	R	C	0	3.64	4.53	3.16

[a]GBp (Greatest Proximal Breadth in Proximal Plane); GD (Greatest Depth); DL (Dorsal Length).

Table 38. Ulnar carpal

Prov.	Side	Port.	But.	[a]GB
E-2/3	R	C	0	3.11
F-9/S	R	C	0	2.57
F-9/35E	L	C	0	2.60
G-6/2	L	C	0	2.97
H-11/3C	L	C	0	(2.40)
H-14/4B	R	C	0	2.95
O-3/39	R	C	0	2.55
P-2/19	L	C	0	2.81
P-4/24	L	C	0	[b]1.72

[a]GB (Greatest Breadth) (after von den Driesch 1976).
[b]From immature individual.

Table 39. Accessory carpal

Prov.	Side	Port.	But.	[a]GB	[a]GL	[a]GD
E-2/12	(L)	C	0	2.01	2.66	2.70
EF-9,10/S	R	C	0	1.72	2.62	2.51
EF-9,10/S	R	C	0	1.63	2.32	2.48
F-9/35A	L	C	0	1.66	2.64	2.57
G-13/7	(L)	C	0	2.51	3.42	3.23
H-14/1B	R	C	0	2.05	2.98	3.14
H-14/15	(L)	C	0	2.55	3.46	3.39
P-2/18	L	C	0	1.83	2.66	2.65
P-3/22	(L)	C	0	1.49	2.56	2.18

[a]GB (Greatest Breadth); GL (Greatest Length); GD (Greatest Depth, measured perpendicular to articular surface).

Table 40. Fused 2nd and 3rd carpal

Prov.	Side	Port.	But.	[a]GB
[b]Bkdt	R	C	0	(4.30)
F-9/35G	L	C	0	3.76
F-9/44B	R	C	0	3.77
H-11/3B	L	C	0	(3.60)
0-4/22	R	C	0	4.14
P-2/7	L	C	0	4.15
P-3/21	R	C	0	4.02
P-3/39	L	Da	0	[3.97]

[a]GB (Greatest Breadth) (after von den Driesch 1976).
[b]From Units EF-13,22.

Table 41. 4th carpal

Prov.	Side	Port.	But.	[a]GB	[b]GL
F-9/35B	L	C	0	3.10	2.47
F-9/35C	L	C	0	2.83	2.49
F-9/44A	R	C	0	3.12	2.48
GH-16/Blk	L	C	0	2.96	2.58
GH-19,20/S	R	C	0	3.09	2.55
H-14/4A	R	C	0	3.77	3.01
P-2/6	L	C	0	3.25	2.72
P-3/16	L	C	0	3.80	3.09
P-3,4/S½/S	R	C	0	3.64	2.93
P-3,4/S½/S	---	Da	0	---	---

[a]GB (Greatest Breadth) (after von den Driesch 1976).
[b]GL (Greatest Length).

Table 42. 5th metacarpal

Prov.	Side	Port.	But.	[a]GB	[a]GL
EF-9,10/S	R	C	0	1.03	3.15
F-9/35D	L	C	0	0.96	3.50
OP-2,4/SA	L	C	0	1.06	4.60
OP-2,4/SB	---	C	0	1.22	[2.91]
P-2/17	L	C	0	1.12	3.98
P-3,4/S½/S	---	Da	0	1.02	[2.32]
P-4/28 (Assoc.)	---	C	0	0.94	2.77

[a]GB (Greatest Breadth); GL (Greatest Length).

Table 43. Metacarpal

Prov.	Side	Port.	But.	Fus. (P)	Fus. (D)	[a]GL	[a]Bp	[a]SD	[a]DD	[a]Bd	[b]WCm	[b]WCl	[b]WTm	[b]WTl
A-2/2B	R	De	0	---	0	[4.06]	---	---	---	(6.63)	3.11	(2.92)	2.69	2.56
D-12/2	(L)	P	[c](1)	(1)	---	[9.80]	[4.54]	---	---	---	---	---	---	---
F-5/1	R	C	0	1	1	(19.53)	5.92	3.60	2.27	6.26	(3.00)	(2.81)	2.63	2.36
F-9/18	L	C	0	1	1	21.00	6.25	3.69	2.41	6.59	3.00	2.92	2.67	2.41
F-9/40	R	C	0	1	1	20.00	6.27	3.73	2.42	6.57	3.05	2.94	2.66	2.36
F-10/14	(L)	P	1	1	---	[8.04]	[3.72]	---	---	---	---	---	---	---
G-10/1	(R)	[d]P,Di	0	(1)	0	[10.31]	3.86	2.40	1.57	---	---	---	---	---
G-15/1	---	[e]Di	(1)	---	---	[6.83]	---	1.68	(1.18)	---	---	---	---	---
H-11/2	L	Da	0	1	0	(19.85)	[5.07]	(3.50)	2.44	[5.81]	(3.12)	---	(2.65)	---
H-14/3	R	C	0	1	1	21.00	7.35	4.70	2.73	7.52	3.46	3.50	3.05	2.78
H-18/1	L	De	0	---	0	[3.50]	---	---	---	(6.30)	3.07	2.77	2.65	2.38
O-3/4	R	P	0	1	---	[17.21]	7.30	5.01	3.02	---	---	---	---	---
O-4/22	R	C	[f]0	1	1	21.05	6.98	3.87	2.56	7.08	3.37	3.19	2.88	2.62
P-3/41	L	C	[f]0	1	1	20.65	6.20	3.58	2.43	6.60	3.04	2.88	2.79	2.63
P-3/43	L	C	0	1	1	19.35	6.39	3.87	2.62	6.44	3.04	2.85	2.85	2.61

[a]GL (Greatest Length); Bp (Proximal Breadth); SD (Smallest Breadth of Diaphysis); DD (Smallest Depth of Diaphysis); Bd (Distal Breadth) (after von den Driesch 1976).

[b]WCm (Width of Distal Medial Condyle); WCl (Width of Distal Lateral Condyle); WTm (Width of Distal Medial Trochlea); WTl (Width of Distal Lateral Trochlea) (after Payne 1969).

[c]Identification as metacarpal uncertain; specimen badly weathered.

[d]Proximal end and shaft of immature individual.

[e]Shaft of immature individual; distal end broken off perpendicular to longitudinal axis of bone; trace of depressed fracture near break.

[f]Two flakes of bone spalled from anterior surface of shaft; may be result of *in situ* weathering or use of metacarpal as hammer.

Table 44. Pelvis

Prov.	Side	[a]GL	[a]LA	[a]LS	[a]SH	[a]SB	[a]SC	[a]LFo	[a]GBTc	[a]GBA	[a]GBTi	[a]SBI
E-2/6	[b]R	[34.55]	(8.45)	---	4.82	2.68	12.20	---	---	---	---	---
E-2/18	[c]R	48.20	7.71	12.74	4.21	2.04	10.45	10.25	(44.50)	(25.00)	(22.00)	(15.50)
E-2/19	[d]L	48.23	7.62	13.28	4.07	2.11	10.45	10.61	(44.50)	(25.00)	(22.00)	(15.50)
E-4/1	[e]L	---	---	---	---	---	---	---	---	---	---	---
F-0024/6	[f]L	---	[4.65]	[8.63]	---	---	---	---	---	---	---	---
F-8/5	[g]R	[23.70]	(6.32)	---	3.31	1.60	8.25	---	---	---	---	---
F-8/6	[h]L	43.00	7.02	[7.76]	3.93	2.54	10.35	[8.69]	---	---	---	---
F-9/1	[i]L	---	---	---	---	---	---	---	---	---	---	---
F-12/7	[j]R	---	---	---	---	---	---	---	---	---	---	---
G-11/13	[k]R	---	[3.73]	---	---	---	---	---	---	---	---	---
G-19/3	[l]R	[13.90]	---	---	---	---	---	---	---	---	---	---
G-22/2	[m]R	[14.80]	[2.15]	---	3.74	2.04	9.65	---	---	---	---	---
H-15/3	[n](R)	[10.40]	---	---	---	---	---	---	---	---	---	---
H-16/7	[o]L	[13.70]	---	---	---	---	---	---	---	---	---	---
H-18/18	[p]R	---	[6.05]	---	---	---	---	---	---	---	---	---
O-2/5	[q]R	[16.90]	---	---	---	---	---	---	---	---	---	---
O-3/17	[r]L	[10.47]	---	---	---	---	---	---	---	---	---	---
O-4/20	[s]R	[29.32]	8.36	---	5.57	3.07	13.95	---	---	---	---	---
O-4/21	[t]R	[11.05]	---	---	---	(2.20)	---	---	---	---	---	---
P-2/1	[u]R	[13.82]	---	---	---	---	---	---	---	---	---	---
P-3, 4/S$\frac{1}{2}$/S	[v]R	---	---	---	---	---	---	---	---	---	---	---
Q-002/1	[w]R	[8.41]	---	---	---	---	---	---	---	---	---	---
Q-1/1	[x]---	---	---	---	---	---	---	---	---	---	---	---
Q-3/14	[y]R	[19.68]	7.31	---	---	---	---	---	---	---	---	---
Q-4/S	[z]R	---	---	---	---	---	---	---	---	---	---	---

[a]GL (Greatest Length); LA (Length of Acetabulum); LS (Length of Symphysis); SH (Smallest Height of Ilium Shaft); SB (Smallest Breadth of Ilium Shaft); SC (Smallest Circumference of Ilium Shaft); LFo (Inner Length of Obturator Foramen); GBTc (Greatest Breadth across Coxal Tubers); GBA (Greatest Breadth across Acetabula); GBTi (Greatest Breadth across Ischiatic Tubers); SBI (Smallest Breadth across Bodies of Ischia) (after von den Driesch 1976).

[b]Ilium with acetabulum only; pubis removed at acetabulum through notches; ischium removed just caudally of acetabulum through lesser ischiatic notch; iliac crest and sacral tuber abraded and weathered; ilium and ischium fused; pubis probably fused; coxal tuber fused; fusion of sacral tuber unknown.

Table 44. (cont.)

[c]Complete; sacral tuber damaged; ilium, ischium and pubis fused; coxal tuber unfused and missing; fusion of sacral tuber unknown; ischiatic tuber unfused and missing; match for E-2/19.

[d]Complete; ilium, ischium and pubis fused; coxal tuber unfused and missing; sacral tuber unfused (?) and missing; ischiatic tuber unfused and missing; match for E-2/18.

[e]Isolated, unfused coxal tuber only.

[f]Isolated pubis; exposed in arroyo and weathered.

[g]Acetabulum with adjacent portions of ilium, ischium and pubis; ilium cut at caudal end of shaft; ischium cut at lesser ischiatic notch and at junction of symphyseal branch of pubis with ischium; ilium and ischium fused; pubis probably fused.

[h]Almost complete pelvis; caudal side of obturator foramen opened by cut through symphyseal branch of ischium at junction with pubis; second cranial-caudal cut through ischial tabula beginning at caudal end of obturator foramen; minor breakage at pubic symphysis; sacral tuber damaged; ilium, ischium and pubis fused; coxal tuber fused; fusion of sacral tuber unknown; ischiatic tuber fused.

[i]Fragment of fused coxal tuber and small attached portion of iliac crest.

[j]Fused coxal tuber, adjacent portion of iliac crest and wing.

[k]Cranial branch of pubis only, including portion of acetabulum, symphyseal branch of pubis removed; pubis probably fused.

[l]Fragment of wing of ilium extending from iliac crest to, and including, greater ischiatic notch; lateral border of ilium, coxal tuber and sacral tuber removed; coxal tuber probably fused.

[m]Shaft of ilium only; ischium and pubis detached by cutting acetabulum; iliac wing removed by cut through shaft at cranial end of greater ischiatic notch; ilium and ischium fused; pubis probably fused.

[n]Fragment of wing of ilium only; includes small portion of greater ischiatic notch; iliac crest, coxal tuber, sacral tuber and lateral border removed.

[o]Fragment of wing of ilium only; includes small portion of greater ischiatic notch; iliac crest, coxal tuber, sacral tuber and lateral border removed.

[p]Acetabulum fragment only; ischium detached at acetabular fossa; pubis removed by cutting through midpoint of cranial branch of pubis; ilium detached by cutting through shaft at point where it joins acetabulum; ilium, ischium and pubis fused.

[q]Ischiatic tuber and adjacent portion of ischium only; ischiatic tuber fused; very robust; weathered.

[r]Ischiatic tuber fragment and small portion of adjacent ischium; fusion unknown; badly weathered.

[s]Ilium shaft, acetabulum and cranial branch of pubis only; wing of ilium detached above greater ischiatic notch; ischium detached at acetabulum; pubis cut near midpoint of cranial branch; ilium, ischium and pubis fused.

[t]Ischial shaft (body) fragment only, extending from just caudal of the acetabulum to the caudal end of the obturator foramen.

[u]Coxal tuber and adjacent portion of iliac wing; includes large portion of lateral border; fusion unknown.

Table 44. (cont.)

[v]Isolated, unfused fragment of coxal tuber; damaged.

[w]Fragment of ischium just cranial to ischiatic tuber, including portion of lesser ischiatic notch and obturator foramen.

[x]Small fragment, probably from crest of ischium.

[y]Acetabulum with portion of iliac shaft and remnant of ischiatic shaft; iliac shaft cut at caudal end of greater ischiatic notch; ischium cut at cranial end of lesser ischiatic notch; pubis removed at acetabular fossa; ilium, ischium and pubis fused.

[z]Fragment of cranial branch of pubis, including portion of acetabulum; pubis and ilium appear to be in process of fusing (?).

Table 45. Femur

Prov.	Side	Port.	But.	Fus. (P)	Fus. (D)	[a]GL	[a]GLC	[a]Bp	[a]DC	[a]SD	[a]CD	[a]Bd
B-1/2	L	D	[b]1	---	1	[19.75]	---	---	---	---	---	(12.45)
E-2/7	R	C	0	1	1	42.80	40.50	15.40	5.70	4.70	15.81	11.85
E-8/4	R	C	0	1	1	37.60	36.13	12.55	4.95	4.18	13.79	10.13
F-10/15	R	C	0	1	1	(38.85)	(38.28)	13.05	5.37	(4.48)	(14.58)	(10.35)
F-22/5	---	P	[c]1	(1)	---	---	---	---	---	---	---	---
F-26/1A	R	D	[d]1	---	1	[13.75]	---	---	---	---	---	[8.68]
H-16/4	R	P	[e]1	1	---	[11.10]	---	(14.06)	5.21	---	---	---
H-18/3	L	C	0	1	1	37.59	36.25	12.60	4.91	4.10	13.82	10.12
O-3/30	---	P	[f]1	1	---	[5.57]	---	---	---	---	---	---
P-2/12	L	C	0	[g]0	0	[38.00]	38.00	[10.40]	5.22	3.95	13.30	10.40
[h]P-2/27	R	C	0	1	1	40.00	38.75	12.34	5.33	4.02	13.25	10.25
P-3/60	L	D	[i]1	---	1	[16.50]	---	---	---	---	---	10.15
Q-3/2	---	D	[j]1	---	---	---	---	---	---	---	---	---
QR-3,4/S	---	Pe	[k](1)	0	---	---	---	---	---	---	---	---

[a]GL (Greatest Length); GLC (Greatest Length from Head); Bp (Proximal Breadth); DC (Greatest Depth of Head); SD (Smallest Breadth of Diaphysis); CD (Smallest Circumference of Diaphysis); Bd (Distal Breadth) (after von den Driesch 1976).

[b]Distal end of femur; shaft broken diagonally to form sharp, lateral point; small, flake-like scars on exterior surface of point suggest possible use as chopping or defleshing tool; no polish.

[c]Femoral head only.

[d]Distal end of femur; shaft broken diagonally to form sharp, anterior point; no flake scars or polish on point; extreme distal end broken; trochlea battered.

[e]Trochanter major of femur cut off posteriorly along plane parallel to longitudinal axis of shaft; shaft broken away from proximal end just below head.

[f]Fragment of femoral head only.

[g]Unfused trochanter major missing.

[h]Shaft submitted to Geochron Laboratories, Cambridge, Mass. for radiocarbon analysis (No. GX-5097-G).

[i]Distal end of femur; shaft broken diagonally to form slight anterior point; no flake scars or polish on point; trochlea battered.

[j]Distal condyle fragment; weathered.

[k]Fragment of unfused epiphyseal head only.

Table 46. Patella

Prov.	Side	Port.	But.	GB[a]	GL[a]
B-2/1	R	C	0	[5.50]	6.62
G-18/1	R	Da	0	[5.20]	[6.91]
H-21/1	L	C	0	6.14	7.15
O-3/24	L	C	0	4.96	6.29
Q-4/24	R	C	0	7.25	[6.98]

[a] GB (Greatest Breadth); GL (Greatest Length) (after von den Driesch 1976).

Table 47. Tibia

Prov.	Side	Port.	But.	Fus.(P)	Fus.(D)	[a]GL	[a]Bp	[a]SD	[a]Bd
"BLM"	R	C	[b]0	0.5	1	37.43	(10.17)	(4.42)	(6.62)
C-2/1	L	P	[c]1	1	---	[15.75]	(10.04)	---	---
E-9/39	R	D	[d]1	---	1	[13.91]	---	(4.73)	7.34
E-23/1	L	P	[e](1)	1	---	[15.10]	---	---	---
E-24/3	L	P	1	1	---	[10.14]	[10.68]	---	---
F-0024/4	R	C	0	1	1	(37.10)	(11.07)	(4.91)	7.32
F-10/10	R	C	0	1	1	36.51	10.34	4.18	6.32
G-9/1	L	D	[f](1)	---	1	[34.32]	---	(4.68)	7.27
G-21/3	L	Pe	0	0	---	---	(10.90)	---	---
H-16/2	L	C	0	1	1	35.62	10.36	4.05	6.69
H-17/19	L	C	[g](0)	1	1	40.50	12.09	5.11	7.71
[h]P-3/55	R	C	0	1	1	37.45	(10.18)	4.30	6.48
P-3/70	R	Di	0	0	0	[24.12]	[8.38]	(3.09)	[5.48]
P-3/75	R	Pe	0	0	---	---	(9.71)	---	---

[a]GL (Greatest Length); Bp (Proximal Breadth); SD (Smallest Breadth of Diaphysis); Bd (Distal Breadth) (after von den Driesch 1976).

[b]Proximal end of tibia with projecting tibial crest.

[c]Shaft broken along irregular surface perpendicular to longitudinal axis of bone.

[d]Anterior portion of proximal end with projecting tibial crest.

[e]Proximal end including most of articular surface; tibial crest missing.

[f]Shaft broken along irregular surface perpendicular to longitudinal axis of bone; specimen damaged during excavation.

[g]Elongate; rectangular hole (8.4 cm x 1.2 cm) in shaft just distal of midpoint on posterior face; piece may have been broken out while using tibia as hammer.

[h]Shaft submitted to Geochron Laboratories, Cambridge, Mass. for radiocarbon analysis (No. GX-5099-G).

Table 48. Astragalus

Prov.	Side	Port.	But.	GLl[a]	GLm[a]	Dl[a]	Dm[a]	Bd[a]	GB[a]
E-19/1	L	C	0	7.10	7.06	4.03	4.30	4.83	5.00
E-26/4	L	C	0	7.18	6.80	4.19	4.18	4.97	5.20
F-8/33	R	C	0	7.23	6.51	4.02	4.11	4.64	4.93
F-11/2	L	C	0	7.30	6.74	4.01	4.26	4.77	5.40
H-16/13	L	C	0	7.73	7.20	4.29	4.49	5.03	5.45
P-2/35	L	C	0	7.99	7.62	4.43	4.40	5.34	5.51
P-3/11	R	C	0	7.96	7.50	4.50	4.70	5.31	5.73

[a] GLl (Greatest Length of Lateral Half); GLm (Greatest Length of Medial Half); Dl (Greatest Depth of Lateral Half); Dm (Greatest Depth of Medial Half); Bd (Greatest Breadth of Distal End); GB (Greatest Breadth) (after von den Driesch 1976).

Table 49. Lateral malleolus

Prov.	Side	Port.	But.	[a]GL	[b]GD
A-2/2A	L	C	0	2.74	3.30
E-3/2	L	C	0	2.88	3.66
EF-7,8/S	R	C	0	2.94	4.13
EF-11/SA	L	C	0	2.98	4.07
EF-11/SB	L	C	0	2.67	3.42
F-2/2	R	C	0	2.91	3.68
F-8/16	L	C	0	2.57	3.43
F-8/18	R	C	0	(2.61)	(3.49)
G-12/4	L	C	0	2.63	3.50

[a]GL (Greatest Length, measured perpendicular to GD).
[b]GD (Greatest Depth) (after von den Driesch 1976).

Table 50. Calcaneus

Prov.	Side	Port.	But.	Fus.(P)	[a]GL	[a]GB	[b]APW	[b]TWp	[b]APWp
D-3/1	R	Da	0	1	(13.52)	4.85	5.55	(3.37)	(3.52)
E-9/3	R	C	0	1	14.41	4.86	5.89	3.49	3.88
E-11/5	R	C	0	1	13.73	4.81	5.52	3.57	4.02
F-8/15	R	[c]Ms	1	0	[10.95]	[5.20]	[6.35]	[3.04]	[4.09]
F-8/19	L	C	0	1	13.49	4.85	5.38	3.41	3.91
F-14/4	L	C	0	1	14.32	5.12	5.65	3.68	4.21
G-7/4	R	Da	0	1	(14.00)	4.90	5.50	[3.13]	(3.89)
H-17/4	L	C	0	1	14.35	4.80	5.99	3.83	3.90
0-3/2	R	[d]Ms,D	0	0	[10.90]	[4.25]	5.31	[2.64]	[3.23]
0-3/9	L	C	0	1	15.10	5.40	6.15	3.60	3.89
0-3/31	L	C	0	1	15.35	5.30	6.05	3.92	4.51

[a]GL (Greatest Length); GB (Greatest Breadth) (after von den Driesch 1976).

[b]APW (Anterior-Posterior Width of "Wing"); TWp (Transverse Width of Proximal End); APWp (Anterior-Posterior Width of Proximal End) (after Lorrain 1968).

[c]Unfused proximal epiphysis missing; distal anterior process removed by cleaver-like cut that penetrated to uniform depth of ca. 3 mm across entire anterior-posterior width of calcaneus.

[d]Unfused proximal epiphysis missing.

Table 51. Naviculo-cuboid

Prov.	Side	Port.	But.	[a]L	[a]TW	[a]APW
D-11/6	R	C	0	5.20	6.64	6.31
E-6/4	L	C	0	4.95	5.95	5.67
F-8/17	R	C	0	4.77	5.89	5.74
F-9/7	R	Da	0	(4.08)	[5.44]	[5.12]
F-14/1	R	C	0	4.18	5.70	5.21
H-12/2	R	C	0	4.83	6.64	6.08
H-17/20	L	C	0	4.46	5.78	5.58
H-18/15	L	C	0	4.14	5.56	5.76
I-16/4	L	C	0	4.08	5.43	5.41
I-16/6	L	C	0	3.96	5.63	5.39

[a]L (Length); TW (Transverse Width); APW (Anterior-Posterior Width) (after Lorrain 1968).

Table 52. 1st tarsal

Prov.	Side	Port.	But.	[a]GB	[a]GL	[a]GD
D-11/8	R	C	0	1.33	1.41	1.92
F-8/13	---	C	0	1.10	1.00	1.42

[a]GB (Greatest Breadth); GL (Greatest Length); GD (Greatest Depth).

Table 53. Fused 2nd and 3rd tarsal

Prov.	Side	Port.	But.	GB[a]
D-11/7	R	C	0	3.60
F-8/14	R	C	0	3.03
F-8/26	R	C	0	2.91
F-8/40	L	C	0	2.92

[a] GB (Greatest Breadth) (after von den Driesch 1976).

Table 54. 2nd metatarsal

Prov.	Side	Port.	But.	GB[a]	GL[a]
F-8/11	---	C	0	2.00	1.52

[a] GB (Greatest Breadth); GL (Greatest Length).

Table 55. Metatarsal

Prov.	Side	Port.	But.	Fus. (P)	Fus. (D)	[a]GL	[a]Bp	[a]SD	[a]DD	[a]Bd	[b]WCm	[b]WCl	[b]WTm	[b]WTl
B-11/1	R	C	0	1	1	24.60	4.94	2.77	2.64	5.89	2.66	2.59	2.60	2.34
D-11/5	R	C	0	1	1	25.40	5.79	4.03	3.09	7.14	3.39	3.16	3.09	2.73
E-3/6	L	C	0	1	1	25.81	5.23	2.89	2.83	6.45	3.04	2.89	2.92	2.60
E-10/7	R	C	0	1	[c](1)	23.31	4.76	(2.98)	2.57	5.78	2.71	2.52	2.42	2.18
E-10/8	L	C	0	1	1	26.10	5.35	3.40	2.99	6.49	2.93	2.82	2.81	2.59
E-25/2	L	Rs	[d](1)	1	1	[23.65]	[4.51]	(2.85)	(2.72)	[5.28]	2.71	---	2.63	---
F-8/12	L	C	0	1	1	24.71	4.85	3.08	2.78	5.98	2.82	2.64	2.64	2.33
H-8/1	L	C	[e](1)	1	1	26.58	5.76	(3.85)	3.22	6.84	3.26	3.02	3.09	2.69
0-3/5	L	C	0	1	1	24.89	5.24	3.08	2.78	6.09	2.89	2.70	2.73	2.43
P-3/59	R	De	0	---	0	[3.62]	---	---	---	(5.31)	2.50	2.34	2.32	2.10

[a]GL (Greatest Length); Bp (Proximal Breadth); SD (Smallest Breadth of Diaphysis); DD (Smallest Depth of Diaphysis); Bd (Distal Breadth) (after von den Driesch 1976).

[b]WCm (Width of Distal Medial Condyle); WCl (Width of Distal Lateral Condyle); WTm (Width of Distal Medial Trochlea); WTl (Width of Distal Lateral Trochlea) (after Payne 1969).

[c]Damaged during excavation producing fracture along distal line of fusion.

[d]Specimen consisted of more than 20 restorable fragments; breakage occurred in situ after burial; shattering may have been result of using metatarsal as hammer.

[e]Anterior surface of shaft toward proximal end shattered and spalled; breakage occurred in situ after burial; shattering may have been result of using metatarsal as hammer.

Table 56. [a]Metapodial

Prov.	Side	Port.	But.	Fus. (P)	Fus. (D)	[b]GL	[b]Bp	[b]SD	[b]DD	[b]Bd	[c]WCm	[c]WCl	[c]WTm	[c]WTl
Bkdt	---	[d]D	---	---	---	[3.33]	---	---	---	---	---	---	---	---
P-4/21	(L)	De	0	---	0	[3.11]	---	---	---	(5.20)	(2.35)	(2.16)	(2.32)	(2.10)

[a]Fragments that could not be assigned to metacarpal or metatarsal.

[b]GL (Greatest Length); Bp (Proximal Breadth); SD (Smallest Breadth of Diaphysis); DD (Smallest Depth of Diaphysis); Bd (Distal Breadth) (after von den Driesch 1976).

[c]WCm (Width of Distal Medial Condyle); WCl (Width of Distal Lateral Condyle); WTm (Width of Distal Medial Trochlea); WTl (Width of Distal Lateral Trochlea) (after Payne 1969).

[d]Single distal condyle; width of condyle 2.74; width of trochlea 2.68.

Table 57. 1st phalanx

Prov.	Side	Port.	But.	Fus.	[a]GLpe	[a]Bp	[a]SD	[a]Bd	[a]Dp	[b]DVR	[c]DVRD
[d]Bkdt	"L"	C	0	1	6.71	3.52	3.14	3.61	3.92	(0.33)	L
A-2/1A	"R"	C	0	1	5.97	2.93	2.50	2.77	3.22	---	(R)
D-11/3	"L"	C	0	1	7.06	3.59	3.18	(3.77)	3.97	(0.25)	L
E-8/17	"R"	C	0	1	6.23	3.39	2.93	3.11	3.29	0.28	R
E-16/1	"L"	Da	0	1	(6.37)	---	---	2.88	---	---	(L)
EF-Bkdt	"L"	Da	0	(1)	[6.20]	[3.31]	3.09	3.35	[3.67]	---	---
EF-9,10/S	"L"	Da	0	1	[4.05]	---	---	---	[3.83]	---	---
F-0024/3	---	[e]Di,D	0	0	[4.57]	[2.50]	2.34	2.66	---	---	---
F-8/7	"R"	C	0	1	6.18	2.98	2.75	2.92	3.47	0.06	L
F-8/20A	L,E	C	0	1	6.21	2.94	2.76	2.95	3.53	0.04	R
F-8/21A	R,E	C	0	1	6.43	3.01	2.74	3.00	3.55	0.14	R
F-9/20	F,L,I	C	0	1	6.18	3.37	2.92	3.11	3.40	0.35	R
F-9/21	F,L,E	C	0	1	6.02	3.21	3.06	3.06	3.41	0.02	R
F-10/1	"L"	C	0	1	6.60	3.02	2.70	2.93	3.36	0.01	R
F-10/7	"R"	C	0	1	6.62	3.09	2.68	2.92	3.44	0.10	L
F-10/11	"L"	C	0	1	6.45	2.98	2.49	2.84	3.22	0.05	R
F-14/3	"R"	Da	0	1	(6.18)	(2.77)	2.62	2.94	3.17	0.05	(R)
F-17/1	"R"	C	0	1	6.82	(3.57)	3.07	3.34	3.92	0.08	R
F-18/2	"R"	C	0	1	7.12	3.58	3.09	3.40	3.95	0.38	R
F-19/1	"R"	C	0	1	6.54	2.91	2.61	2.87	3.35	0.07	L
F-21/3	"R"	C	0	1	6.73	3.26	2.83	3.25	(3.48)	---	(R)
F-22/2	"L"	C	0	1	6.92	3.30	3.09	3.36	3.63	0.05	R
F-22/8	"R"	C	0	1	6.19	3.24	3.11	3.26	3.43	0.01	L
F-22/9	"L"	C	0	1	6.30	3.35	3.16	3.27	3.24	0.11	(L)
F-22/Blk	"R"	C	0	1	6.44	(3.44)	2.89	3.24	(3.28)	0.40	R
G-14/5	"R"	C	0	1	6.18	3.28	2.73	2.84	3.36	0.45	R
GH-19,22/SA	"R"	Pe	0	0	---	2.81	---	---	(2.84)	---	---
GH-19,22/SB	---	P,La	(1)	1	---	---	---	---	---	---	---
H-11/1	---	Da	0	1	---	---	---	3.26	---	---	---
H-14/7	"R"	Da	0	1	6.19	(3.27)	---	3.05	3.27	(0.32)	R
H-17/9	"L"	C	0	1	6.34	3.42	2.93	3.30	3.38	(0.32)	L
H-18/8	"L"	C	0	1	6.36	3.02	2.75	3.18	3.49	(0.19)	L
H-20/3	"R"	C	0	1	7.10	3.95	3.30	3.58	3.88	0.43	R
H-21/3	"L"	C	0	1	6.33	3.44	2.96	3.64	3.56	(0.31)	L

Table 57. (cont.)

Prov.	Side	Port.	But.	Fus.	[a]GLpe	[a]Bp	[a]SD	[a]Bd	[a]Dp	[b]DVR	[c]DVRD
0-2/8	"R"	C	0	1	7.43	3.75	3.27	3.60	4.05	0.07	L
0-4/3	"R"	C	0	1	6.82	[4.10]	[3.46]	(3.86)	(3.77)	---	---
0-4/9	"L"	C	0	1	7.25	4.02	3.73	3.93	4.14	0.01	R
P-2/4	"L"	C	0	[f]0	6.80	2.83	(2.43)	2.92	3.49	0.11	R
P-3/47	"L"	C	0	1	6.23	3.25	3.07	3.08	3.52	0.25	L
P-3/48	"R"	C	0	1	6.56	3.45	3.05	3.31	3.59	0.18	L
P-3/57	"R"	C	0	1	5.85	3.32	2.76	3.10	3.30	0.33	R
P-3/78	"L"	C	0	1	7.02	3.98	3.42	3.87	3.89	0.39	L
P-3/80	"R"	C	0	1	7.36	3.61	2.98	3.40	3.88	0.23	R
Q-3/4	"R"	Da	0	1	6.52	(3.76)	(3.39)	3.73	3.75	0.34	R
Q-3/15	"R"	C	0	1	6.85	3.10	2.82	3.16	3.51	0.13	R
Q-3/S	---	Da	0	(1)	[6.19]	---	---	---	---	---	---
Q-4/18	---	[e]Di,D	0	0	[5.23]	[2.53]	2.29	2.78	---	---	---

[a]GLpe (Greatest Length of Peripheral Half); Bp (Proximal Breadth); SD (Smallest Breadth of Diaphysis); Bd (Distal Breadth); Dp (Proximal Depth) (after von den Driesch 1976).

[b]DVR (Distal-Volar Rock); Observed by placing specimen volar surface down and measuring distance of rock as viewed distally (after Duffield 1970:80-81).

[c]DVRD (Distal-Volar Rock Direction); DVR clockwise (Right); DVR counterclockwise (Left).

[d]Extreme west end of Trench EFGH.

[e]Proximal epiphysis missing.

[f]Proximal epiphysis unfused but present.

Table 58. 2nd phalanx

Prov.	Side	Port.	But.	Fus.	^{a}GL	^{a}Bp	^{a}SD	^{a}Bd	^{b}D
Bkdt	"R"	Pe	0	0	---	(2.55)	---	---	---
D-11/2	"L"	C	0	1	4.77	(3.61)	2.60	2.92	2.63
E-2/13	Re,"R"	C	0	1	4.45	3.15	2.40	2.58	2.63
E-2/22	Re,"L"	C	0	1	4.85	3.57	2.50	2.93	2.77
E-20/3	Re,"L"	C	0	1	4.27	3.19	2.38	2.68	(2.40)
E-26/2	(F),"R"	C	0	1	4.18	3.19	2.53	(2.48)	2.15
F-4/7	Re,"R"	C	0	1	4.55	3.13	2.43	2.65	(2.69)
F-6/S	F,"R"	C	0	1	4.49	3.55	2.77	(2.94)	2.32
F-8/20B	R,E	C	0	1	4.26	2.99	2.30	2.46	2.33
F-8/21B	R,I	C	0	1	4.26	3.09	2.32	2.47	2.25
F-9/22	F,L,I	C	0	1	4.10	3.22	2.60	2.52	1.97
F-9/23	F,L,E	C	0	1	4.11	3.23	2.50	2.64	1.99
F-10/5	"R"	Da	0	1	4.19	3.21	2.45	[2.76]	[2.01]
F-10/9	("L")	Di,D	0	^{c}0	[2.86]	[2.54]	2.10	2.46	---
F-10/12	Re,"R"	C	0	1	4.22	2.96	2.24	2.39	2.44
F-21/2	Re,"L"	C	0	1	4.69	3.36	2.49	2.81	2.73
G-11/4	Re,"L"	C	0	1	4.73	(3.44)	2.49	2.86	2.67
G-19/1	F,"R"	C	0	1	4.30	3.54	2.87	3.03	2.08
G-21,22/S	Re,"R"	C	0	1	4.80	3.42	2.67	(2.83)	2.87
G-21,22/S	(Re),"R"	C	0	1	4.69	3.37	2.70	2.76	2.62
G-22/4	"R"	C	0	1	[4.49]	(3.62)	2.94	(3.06)	2.49
GH-19,22/S	Re,"L"	C	0	1	4.83	3.55	2.75	2.90	2.73
H-10/2	(Re),"L"	C	0	1	4.66	3.62	2.58	(3.13)	(2.65)
H-11,12/S	("L")	Da	0	1	---	---	---	---	---
H-14/12	F,"L"	C	0	1	4.30	(3.09)	2.39	(2.52)	2.27
H-14/13	F,"L"	C	0	1	4.76	3.88	3.00	3.29	2.42
O-3/29	Re,"L"	C	0	1	4.46	2.92	2.18	2.43	2.82
QP-2,4/S	"R"	Pe	0	0	---	(2.67)	---	---	---
P-2/14	F,"L"	C	0	1	4.87	3.84	2.94	3.47	2.51
P-3/82	(Re),"L"	Da	0	1	4.53	2.91	(2.27)	2.45	---
P-4/18	Re,"L"	C	0	1	4.98	3.54	2.70	2.92	2.87
P-4/20	F,"R"	C	0	1	4.28	3.43	2.70	2.98	2.08
Q-3/17	F,"L"	C	0	1	4.61	3.89	3.06	3.41	2.31
Q-4/16	Re,"R"	C	0	1	4.34	2.85	2.10	(2.11)	2.45
QR-5,6/S	"L"	Da	0	1	[3.69]	---	[2.39]	[2.61]	---

Table 58. (cont.)

[a]GL (Greatest Length); Bp (Proximal Breadth); SD (Smallest Breadth of Diaphysis); Bd (Distal Breadth) (after von den Driesch 1976).

[b]D (Dorsal Length) (after Duffield 1970:81).

[c]Proximal epiphysis missing.

Table 59. 3rd phalanx

Prov.	Side	Port.	But.	[a]DLS	[a]Ld	[a]MBS
[b]Bkdt	"R"	C	0	8.26	[6.00]	2.73
E-2/15	"L"	C	0	8.73	6.57	2.81
E-6/1	"R"	C	0	7.50	(6.33)	2.72
E-23/7	"R"	C	0	7.50	6.21	2.36
EF-9,10/S	"R"	[c]C	0	3.10	[2.74]	(1.18)
F-2/3	"L"	C	0	5.87	5.02	2.07
F-8/13	"R"	C	0	6.75	5.80	2.24
F-8/34A	"R"	C	0	6.50	5.50	2.20
F-9/24	F,L,I	C	0	7.58	5.69	2.50
F-9/25	F,L,E	C	0	7.30	5.65	2.62
F-9/32	"L"	C	0	6.87	5.89	2.31
F-9/43	"L"	C	0	6.42	5.54	2.37
F-10/24	"R"	C	0	(7.19)	5.47	2.60
F-21/1	"L"	C	0	(7.35)	(5.24)	(3.06)
F-22/3	"R"	C	0	7.38	6.38	2.43
F-24/7	"R"	Da	0	6.31	[5.13]	(2.08)
G-11/8	"L"	C	0	7.42	5.60	(2.51)
G-11/9	"L"	C	0	(6.84)	(5.74)	2.27
G-11/12	"R"	C	0	7.67	6.16	2.64
G-18/3	"L"	Da	0	[6.66]	5.85	2.68
G-19/2	"R"	C	0	8.23	6.40	3.14
GH-7,8/S	"R"	C	0	6.64	5.54	2.41
H-16/12	"L"	C	0	7.21	6.04	2.30
H-18/2	"L"	C	0	6.63	5.81	2.50
H-21/6	"L"	C	0	5.94	4.77	2.06
0-2/3	"L"	C	0	8.20	6.40	3.27
0-2/10	"R"	Da	0	[6.46]	[5.44]	(2.29)
0-4/8	"R"	C	0	7.08	5.62	2.30
0-4/14	"R"	C	0	6.19	5.11	2.18
0P-2,4/S	"L"	C	0	7.74	6.55	2.84
P-3/6	"L"	Da	0	[6.76]	[5.15]	2.32
P-3/8	"R"	C	0	8.13	6.24	2.83
P-3/14	"R"	C	0	7.69	6.45	(2.45)
P-3/27	"L"	C	0	6.46	5.22	2.27
P-3/61	"R"	C	0	6.97	5.80	2.67

Table 59. (cont.)

Prov.	Side	Port.	But.	[a]DLS	[a]Ld	[a]MBS
Q-3/16	"R"	C	0	7.78	5.84	2.85
Q-3/18	"L"	C	[d](1)	(6.53)	(5.50)	2.26
Q-3/24	"R"	Da	0	[6.87]	[5.38]	2.73
Q-4/15	"R"	C	0	7.09	5.99	2.35
Q-4/32	"R"	Vo	[e](1)	[4.28]	[3.23]	(2.50)
Q-4/S	"R"	Da	0	[7.42]	---	[2.52]

[a]DLS (Greatest Diagonal Length of Sole); Ld (Length of Dorsal Surface); MBS (Middle Breadth of Sole) (after von den Driesch 1976).

[b]Extreme west end of Trench EFGH.

[c]From immature individual.

[d]Longitudinal break (pieces still attached).

[e]Transverse break near midsection.

Table 60. Proximal sesamoid

Prov.	Side	Port.	But.	a_{GB}	a_{GL}	a_{GD}
D-11/4	"L",P	C	0	1.87	2.37	2.45
E-4/2	"R",P	C	0	1.72	2.21	2.26
E-5,6/S	("R"),C	C	0	1.38	2.66	1.61
E-7/S	"L",C	Da	0	[1.97]	[2.71]	[2.07]
E-8/27	"L",P	C	0	(1.54)	1.98	1.77
E-9/S	"L",C	C	0	1.52	2.38	1.47
E-11/4	"R",P	C	0	1.66	2.18	(1.89)
EF-9,10/S	"R",P	C	0	1.51	2.03	2.25
EF-19,20/S	"R",C	C	0	1.83	[2.98]	2.00
EF-19,20/S	"L",C	C	0	1.58	[2.43]	[1.66]
EF-21,22/S	"L",P	C	0	1.66	2.11	2.04
EF-22/S	"L",P	C	0	1.51	2.08	2.07
EF-24/S	"R",C	C	0	2.06	3.19	2.21
F-0024/14	"R",C	C	0	1.92	2.81	2.03
F-8/27	"R",P	C	0	1.76	2.15	2.40
F-8/35	"R",C	C	0	1.54	2.40	1.42
F-9/19A	"L",C	C	0	1.76	2.50	1.63
F-9/19B	"R",C	C	0	1.62	2.56	1.63
F-9/19C	"L",P	C	0	1.71	2.34	1.99
F-9/19D	"R",P	C	0	1.62	2.21	2.07
F-9/41	"L",C	C	0	1.64	(2.58)	(1.60)
F-9/42	"L",P	C	0	1.53	2.18	2.07
F-10/6	"R",C	C	0	1.52	2.49	1.55
F-10/26	"R",C	C	0	1.67	2.59	1.77
F-20/1	"L",C	C	0	(1.69)	(2.71)	(1.72)
F-22/4	"L",P	C	0	1.62	(2.22)	2.18
F-26/1C	"R",P	Da	0	(1.68)	[2.42]	[2.36]
G-11/10	("R"),C	Da	0	1.56	[2.35]	[1.36]
G-11,12/S	"R",P	Da	0	(1.60)	[2.18]	[1.87]
G-16/5	"L",P	C	0	1.64	2.10	2.12
G-21,22/S	"R",P	C	0	1.52	2.14	2.13
H-11,12/S	"L",P	C	0	1.67	2.12	2.12
H-14/16A	"R",C	C	0	1.60	2.51	1.70
H-14/16B	"L",C	C	0	1.66	2.60	1.71
H-16,18/S	"R",C	C	0	1.64	2.61	1.75

Table 60. (cont.)

Prov.	Side	Port.	But.	[a]GB	[a]GL	[a]GD
0-2/8	"L",P	C	0	1.68	2.10	2.15
0-4/11	"R",P	C	0	1.89	2.71	2.42
OP-2,4/SA	"L",P	C	0	1.43	1.94	1.92
OP-2,4/SB	"L",P	C	0	1.27	(2.19)	(2.05)
OP-2,4/SC	"L",P	C	0	1.09	(1.74)	1.59
OP-2,4/SAA	"L",C	C	0	1.55	2.35	1.53
OP-2,4/SBB	"L",P	C	0	1.55	2.13	1.93
P-2/29	"L",P	C	0	1.74	2.17	2.30
P-2/33	"R",C	C	0	1.82	2.92	1.98
P-2/34	"L",C	C	0	1.47	2.49	1.57
P-3/15	"R",C	C	0	1.50	2.50	1.62
P-3/53	"L",P	C	0	1.65	2.33	2.00
P-4/26	"L",C	C	0	1.81	2.88	2.06
Q-3/9	"L",P	C	0	1.71	2.25	2.13
Q-4/29	"L",P	C	0	1.65	2.25	2.29
Q-4/30	"R",P	C	0	1.42	1.90	1.81
Q-4/31	"L",P	C	0	1.85	2.70	2.22

[a]GB (Greatest Breadth); GL (Greatest Length); GD (Greatest Depth).

Table 61. Distal sesamoid

Prov.	Side	Port.	But.	[a]GB	[a]GL	[a]GD
B-1/1	"L"	C	0	2.85	[1.54]	(1.61)
E-2/10	"L"	C	0	2.97	1.74	1.50
E-7/4	"R"	C	0	2.45	(1.40)	(1.22)
E-9/S	"L"	C	0	2.45	1.52	1.23
EF-1,3/S	"R"	C	0	2.49	1.48	1.31
EF-5,6/S	"R"	Da	0	[2.34]	(1.27)	(1.24)
EF-7,8/S	"R"	Da	0	[2.40]	1.68	(1.55)
F-8/8	"R"	C	0	2.43	1.55	1.25
F-8/9	"R"	C	0	2.45	1.55	1.22
F-8/24	"L"	C	0	2.33	1.34	1.11
F-9/SA	"L"	C	0	2.46	1.60	1.33
F-9/SB	"R"	C	0	2.49	[1.62]	1.29
F-9,10/S	"L"	C	0	2.30	(1.27)	1.09
G-10/2	"R"	C	0	2.96	2.03	1.54
GH-15/Blk	"L"	C	0	2.40	1.37	1.11
GH-19,22/S	"R"	C	0	2.88	1.80	1.65
GH-19,22/S	"L"	C	0	2.58	1.63	1.43
I-16/7	"L"	C	0	2.46	1.49	1.22
P-3/50	"L"	Da	0	2.49	1.59	[1.30]
Q-4/20	("R")	Da	0	[1.39]	[1.45]	[1.07]
QR-5,6/S	"L"	C	0	2.78	1.44	1.34

[a]GB (Greatest Breadth); GL (Greatest Length); GD (Greatest Depth).

Table 62. [a]Unidentifiable bone fragments

Prov.	No.	Wt. (g)	Comments
C-2/S (Z=128)	4	8.9	
D-10/2	1	28.9	[b]LBF
D-11,12/S (7/11/77)	9	5.7	
D-12/S (7/10/77)	7	4.1	
E-1/S (5/31/77)	1	4.0	
E-1/11	1	4.3	
E-2/9	1	47.1	LBF
E-2/14	2	37.0	2 LBF
E-2/21	1	4.5	
E-3/4	1	5.9	LBF
E-3/10	1	1.9	LBF
E-3/13	1	3.6	LBF; waterworn (?)
E-3/14	1	8.2	Cartilage (?)
E-3,4/S (6/4/77)	7	6.9	1 waterworn
E-3,4/S (6/5/77)	7	5.2	
E-8/5	4	6.6	
E-9/S (6/14/77)	4	2.6	
E-10/2	1	6.9	LBF; burned
E-10/3	1	44.4	LBF; mineralized (?)
E-11/S (6/27/77)	2	3.8	1 waterworn
E-15/1	1	18.1	LBF (ulna?)
E-16/2	1	46.3	LBF
E-19/S(Blk) (7/29/77)	1	1.8	
E-19/2	1	1.7	
E-20/1	1	2.9	
E-20/3A	1	0.5	
E-22/2	1	4.3	
E-26/5 & E-27/1	1	5.5	LBF
EF-1,2/S (Z=122-132)	1	2.8	LBF
EF-1,2/S (5/30/77)	14	36.2	4 LBF
EF-1,2/S (5/31/77)	3	4.3	
EF-1,2/S (5/31/77)	2	12.8	
EF-3,4/S (5/30/77)	6	15.8	3 LBF
EF-5,6/S (6/5/77)	1	2.8	LBF
EF-5,6/S (6/6/77)	14	24.3	3 LBF

Table 62. (cont.)

Prov.	No.	Wt.(g)	Comments
EF-5,6/S (6/7/77)	6	12.2	1 LBF
EF-5,6/S (Z=98)	4	12.1	1 LBF
EF-7,8/S (Z=98)	1	2.6	LBF
EF-7,8/S (5/31/77)	2	4.8	
EF-7,8/S (6/5/77)	3	3.8	2 waterworn
EF-7,8/S (6/6/77)	9	13.5	1 LBF; 1 waterworn
EF-9,10/S (6/10/77)	3	13.6	1 LBF; 1 waterworn
EF-9,10/S (6/12/77)	4	8.2	2 LBF; 1 waterworn
EF-9,10/S (6/13/77)	2	8.9	1 LBF
EF-9,10/S (6/14/77)	8	7.3	1 waterworn
EF-9,10/S (6/16/77)	15	15.9	3 LBF; 5 waterworn; 1 burned
EF-9,10/S (6/18/77)	1	0.9	
EF-9,10/S (6/26/77)	7	14.9	2 waterworn
EF-11/S (6/28/77)	9	11.0	3 LBF
EF-11/S (7/1/77)	3	2.4	
EF-11,12/S (6/26/77)	2	8.1	
EF-13,14/S (6/26/77)	4	19.5	1 LBF
EF-16,18/S (6/15/77)	1	2.8	
EF-16,18/S (6/27/77)	2	4.6	
EF-17,18/S (6/26/77)	1	14.9	LBF
EF-21,22/S (7/16/77)	1	3.4	
EF-22/S (7/25/77)	3	13.5	3 LBF
EF-22/S (7/26/77)	2	5.0	2 LBF
EF-23,26/S (7/12/77)	1	1.5	
EF-23,26/S (7/23/77)	2	22.3	1 LBF
EF-23,26/S (7/25/77)	1	7.2	LBF
EF-25,26/S (7/18/77)	1	2.2	LBF
F-1/A (lower gravel)	1	8.6	LBF
F-1/2	1	6.4	
F-1,2/S (lower gravel)	2	4.8	
F-1,2/S (5/28/77)	1	2.0	
F-3/3	1	22.9	LBF
F-3/5	1	4.5	
F-3/S (6/3/77)	3	2.4	
F-4/1	2	3.2	

Table 62. (cont.)

Prov.	No.	Wt.(g)	Comments
F-5/4	1	0.3	
F-7/1	1	1.3	
F-7/S (5/30/77)	1	1.3	
F-8/23	1	10.9	LBF
F-9/3	1	1.8	
F-9/36	1	0.6	
F-9/44	2	1.8	
F-9/52	1	1.1	
F-10/2	2	5.0	
F-10/13	1	4.8	
F-10/25	1	4.7	
F-10/28	1	12.6	LBF
F-16/S (6/26/77)	1	4.7	
F-18/1	1	8.9	LBF (metapodial?)
F-20/2	1	7.3	LBF
F-22/11 & 12	2	9.1	2 LBF
F-24/14	1	2.9	Scapula (?)
F-26/1A	1	13.4	LBF (femur head?)
F-26/1B	1	10.4	LBF
F-0024/S (misc.)	12	38.5	Screening of talus deposit below skull F-0024/1
G-2/1	1	0.8	
G-5,6/S (6/4/77)	6	14.3	2 LBF
G-15,18/Blk (8/2/77)	1	4.4	LBF
G-16/2	1	4.2	
G-16/3	2	3.0	
G-16/4	1	1.8	
G-19/3	2	2.2	
G-19/6	1	1.1	
G-19/8	1	4.8	
G-20/3	1	3.2	
G-20/4	1	5.6	Scapula (?)
G-20/5	1	1.4	
G-22/9	1	16.0	LBF (ulna?)
G-21,22/S (8/3/77)	5	3.4	
GH-9,10/S (7/12/77)	3	5.0	

Table 62. (cont.)

Prov.	No.	Wt.(g)	Comments
GH-11,12/S (7/12/77)	5	5.7	2 waterworn
GH-11,12/S (7/15/77)	3	9.2	1 LBF
GH-11,12/S (7/16/77)	14	34.6	1 LBF; 1 burned
GH-11,12/S (7/17/77)	1	0.3	
GH-12,13/S (7/11/77)	2	4.3	
GH-13,14/S (7/11/77)	7	5.0	
GH-13,14/S (7/12/77)	4	4.8	
GH-13,14/S (7/15/77)	4	13.9	1 LBF
GH-13,14/S (7/16/77)	2	4.4	1 LBF
GH-14,15/S (7/9/77)	4	5.8	
GH-15/S (Blk) (7/29/77)	7	6.5	
GH-16,18/S (7/12/77)	4	5.7	1 LBF
GH-16,19/S (7/5/77)	5	8.2	
GH-16/S (7/4/77)	10	15.0	1 LBF
GH-16/S (7/9/77)	3	3.2	
GH-16/S (7/19/77)	4	6.3	
GH-16,18/S (7/8/77)	1	2.8	
GH-17/S (7/4/77)	7	7.9	
GH-17/S (7/9/77)	7	6.2	
GH-18/S (7/9/77)	1	2.4	
GH-18/S (7/17/77)	1	5.2	LBF
GH-19,22/S (7/15/77)	4	16.1	
GH-19,22/S (7/22/77)	3	2.7	
GH-19,22/S (7/23/77)	6	6.4	
GH-19,22/S (7/25/77	1	0.1	Burned
GH-19,22/S (7/26/77)	2	0.9	
GH-19,20/S (8/3/77)	4	1.9	1 rod-like fragment (hyoid?)
H-5/S (7/22/77)	2	4.1	
H-9,10/S (6/14/77)	1	1.0	
H-11/2	1	2.4	
H-11,12/S (7/3/77)	3	2.1	
H-12/S (7/17/77)	2	2.1	
H-11,12/S (7/18/77)	3	6.2	
H-14/8	1	6.8	
H-16/S (7/11/77) (S. Wall)	2	3.8	
H-16/S (7/15/77)	1	3.1	

Table 62. (cont.)

Prov.	No.	Wt. (g)	Comments
H-16/1	1	30.4	LBF
H-16/9	1	10.5	
H-16/11	1	11.2	
H-17/15	1	6.3	LBF
H-18/11	1	1.8	
H-17,18/S (7/10/77)	2	1.8	
H-19/1	c30	20.1	
I-5/1	1	8.9	LBF
O-2/9	1	0.6	
O-2/12	1	3.4	
O-2/13	1	7.6	
O-3/10	1	2.9	
O-3/32	1	5.3	
O-3/35	1	5.5	
O-3/37	1	1.2	
O-3,4/arroyo talus	5	29.8	2 LBF; badly weathered
OP-2,4/S (7/30/77)	5	13.2	2 LBF
OP-2,4/S (8/1/77)	12	17.0	2 LBF
OP-2,4/S (8/4/77)	8	5.3	
OP-2,4/S (8/5/77)	21	21.0	2 rod-like fragments (hyoid?)
OP-2,4/S (8/8/77)	3	9.2	2 LBF
OP-2,4/S (8/9/77)	13	12.3	1 rod-like fragment (hyoid?)
OP-2,4/S (8/10/77)	6	17.4	1 LBF
OP-2,4/S (8/11/77)	2	8.4	1 LBF
P-2/36	1	4.7	LBF
P-3/2	1	2.3	LBF
P-3/7	1	5.9	LBF
P-3/24	1	15.1	LBF
P-3/25	1	8.3	LBF
P-3/51	1	5.2	LBF
P-3/67	1	2.3	
P-3/69	1	2.2	
P-3/74	1	5.2	LBF
P-3/75	1	8.9	LBF
P-3,4/S (N. Wall)	1	5.3	LBF

Table 62. (cont.)

Prov.	No.	Wt.(g)	Comments
P-3,4/S½/S (6/11/77)	9	16.6	1 LBF
P-3,4/S (6/12/77)	1	3.2	LBF; slightly waterworn
P-4/2	1	7.1	
P-4/19	1	4.4	
P-4/30	1	3.3	
Q-1/1	1	1.6	
Q-2/S (N. Wall)(6/5/77)	1	15.8	
Q-2/Blk (6/13/77)	1	4.8	
Q-3/6	1	35.7	LBF
Q-3/10	2	5.1	
Q-3/S (6/6/77)	4	5.3	
Q-4/4	1	2.1	
Q-4/6	1	4.4	
Q-4/17	1	3.1	
Q-4/21	2	3.1	
Q-4/25	2	2.8	
Q-6/3	1	7.1	
QR-001,002/S (6/12/77)	1	1.6	
QR-001,002/S (6/13/77)	1	6.5	LBF
QR-3,4/S (6/4/77)	8	11.1	2 rod-like fragments (hyoids?)

[a]Unidentifiable bone fragments with one or more old breaks (butchering debris); some of these fragments undoubtedly represent natural disintegration products.

[b]LBF (Long-Bone Fragment).

[c]Only largest fragments are included; more than 60 additional tiny fragments were discarded; fragments were found in concentrated deposit probably representing fill of old rodent burrow; none were identifiable.

APPENDIX II. SNAILS FROM THE GARNSEY SITE

Table 63. [a]Snails

Prov.	No.	[b]Comment
"BLM"	1	C
Arroyo Profile/Geol/E	1	P
G-13,14/S (7/11/77)	1	P
H-11,12/S (7/18/77)	1	C
[c]H-14/S (7/12/77)	1	U
0-3/40	1	C
OP-2,4/S (7/29/77)	1	C
OP-2,4/S (7/29/77)	1	U
OP-2,4/S (7/30/77)	2	P
P-2/20	1	U
P-2/30	1	U
P-3/34	1	P
P-3/58	1	P

[a]Identifications by Robert Hanley, Collection Manager, Mollusc Division, Museum of Zoology, University of Michigan; stratigraphic context of snails has not yet been evaluated.

[b]C (*Catinella* cf. *avara*, Family Succinidae); P (*Physa virgata* Gould, Family Physidae); U (Unidentifiable); *C. avara* is amphibious, inhabiting permanently moist areas; *P. virgata* inhabits rocky substrates or macrophytic vegetation up to one meter below surface in freshwater streams, ponds or lakes (McMahon 1975:1167).

[c]Associated with H-14/10.

REFERENCES CITED

Bedord, Jean Newman
1974 Morphological Variation in Bison Metacarpals and Metatarsals. In: The Casper Site, edited by George C. Frison, pp. 199-240. New York: Academic Press.

Binford, Lewis R.
1963 A Proposed Attribute List for the Description and Classification of Projectile Points. Museum of Anthropology, University of Michigan, Anthropological Paper 19:193-221.

Brézillon, Michel N.
1971 La Dénomination des Objets de Pierre Taillée. Gallia-Préhistoire, Supplément IV.

Collins, Michael B.
1966 The Andrews Lake Sites: Evidence of Semi-Sedentary Prehistoric Occupation in Andrews County, Texas. Midland Archaeological Society Bulletin 1:27-43.
1971 A Review of Llano Estacado Archeology and Ethnohistory. Plains Anthropologist 16:85-104.

Dillehay, Tom D.
1974 Late Quaternary Bison Population Changes on the Southern Plains. Plains Anthropologist 19:180-96.

von den Driesch, Angela
1976 A Guide to the Measurement of Animal Bones from Archaeological Sites Peabody Museum of Archaeology and Ethnology, Harvard University, Peabody Museum Bulletin 1.

Duffield, Lathel F.
1970 Some Panhandle Aspect Sites: Their Vertebrates and Paleoecology. Unpublished Ph.D. Dissertation. University of Wisconsin, Madison.

Ferguson, George A.
1966 Statistical Analysis in Psychology and Education (2nd ed.). New York: McGraw-Hill.

Frison, George C.
1968 A Functional Analysis of Certain Chipped Stone Tools. American Antiquity 33:149-55.

Frison, George C., Michael Wilson, and Diane Wilson
1976 Fossil Bison and Artifacts from an Early Altithermal Period Arroyo Trap in Wyoming. American Antiquity 41:28-57.

Frison, George C., Michael Wilson, and Danny N. Walker
1978 The Big Goose Creek Site: Bison Procurement and Faunal Analysis. Occasional Papers on Wyoming Archeology 1.

REFERENCES CITED

Greer, John W.
1976 Notes on Bison in Val Verde County, Texas: Additions to Dillehay. _Plains Anthropologist_ 21:237-39.

Guthrie, R.D.
1966 Pelage of Fossil Bison--A New Osteological Index. _Journal of Mammalogy_ 47:725-27.

Jelinek, Arthur J.
1967 A Prehistoric Sequence in the Middle Pecos Valley, New Mexico. _Museum of Anthropology, University of Michigan, Anthropological Paper_ 31.

Kelley, Vincent C.
1971 Geology of the Pecos Country, Southeastern New Mexico. _New Mexico State Bureau of Mines and Mineral Resources Memoir_ 24.

Lorrain, Dessamae
1968 Analysis of the Bison Bones from Bonfire Shelter. In: Bonfire Shelter: A Stratified Bison Kill Site, Val Verde County, Texas, by David Dibble and Dessamae Lorrain, pp. 77-138. _Texas Memorial Museum, Miscellaneous Paper_ 1.

McMahon, Robert F.
1975 Effects of Artificially Elevated Water Temperatures on the Growth, Reproduction and Life Cycle of a Natural Population of _Physa virgata_ Gould. _Ecology_ 56:1167-75.

Payne, Sebastian
1969 A Metrical Distinction Between Sheep and Goat Metacarpals. In: _The Domestication and Exploitation of Plants and Animals_, edited by Peter J. Ucko and G.W. Dimbleby, pp. 295-306. Chicago: Aldine.

Ralph, E.K., H.N. Michael, and M.C. Han
1973 Radiocarbon Dates and Reality. _MASCA Newsletter_ 9:1-20.

Reed, Erik K.
1955 Bison Beyond the Pecos. _Texas Journal of Science_ 4:130-35.

Reher, Charles A.
1974 Population Study of the Casper Site Bison. In: _The Casper Site_, edited by George C. Frison, pp. 113-24. New York: Academic Press.
1977 Adaptive Process on the Shortgrass Plains. In: _For Theory Building in Archaeology_, edited by Lewis R. Binford, pp. 13-40. New York: Academic Press.

Runyan, John W., and John A. Hedrick
1973 Pottery Types of the SWFAS Area. _Transactions of the Eighth Regional Archaeological Symposium for Southeastern New Mexico and Western Texas_: 19-45.

REFERENCES CITED

Shackleton, D.M., L.V. Hills, and D.A. Hutton
1975 Aspects of Variation in Cranial Characters of Plains Bison (*Bison Bison Bison* Linnaeus) from Elk Island National Park, Alberta. *Journal of Mammalogy* 56:871-87.

Skinner, Morris F., and Ove C. Kaisen
1947 The Fossil *Bison* of Alaska and Preliminary Revision of the Genus. *American Museum of Natural History Bulletin* 89:123-256.

Speth, John D.
1978 The Role of Platform Angle and Core Size in Hard-Hammer Percussion Flaking. In: *Lithic Analysis in Archaeology*, edited by Ruth E. Tringham. New York: Academic Press.

White, Leslie A.
1942 The Pueblo of Santa Ana, New Mexico. *American Anthropological Association Memoir* 60.

Wilmsen, Edwin N.
1970 Lithic Analysis and Cultural Inference: A Paleo-Indian Case. *University of Arizona*, *Anthropological Paper* 16.

Wilson, Michael
1974 The Casper Local Fauna and its Fossil Bison. In: *The Casper Site*, edited by George C. Frison, pp. 125-71. New York: Academic Press.

Wobst, H. Martin
1975 Computers and Coordinates: Strategies for the Analysis of Paleolithic Stratigraphy. Unpublished manuscript on file at the Department of Anthropology, University of Massachusetts.

www.ingramcontent.com/pod-product-compliance
Lightning Source LLC
LaVergne TN
LVHW080303260826
846302LV00007B/28
9780932206732